Destination
HEARTLAND:
183 DEVOTIONALS *to* PLANT IN 365 DAYS

Demario L. Rollins

Destination
HEARTLAND:
183 Devotionals to Plant in 365 Days

"Still other seeds fell on fertile soil, and they sprouted, grew, and produced a crop that was thirty, sixty, and even a hundred times as much as had been planted!" (**Mark 4:8 NLT**)

XULON PRESS

Xulon Press
2301 Lucien Way #415
Maitland, FL 32751
407.339.4217
www.xulonpress.com

Dedications:

To the **Author of Life** itself, You gave it ALL for me. If I could but grant a moment of this life to offer you mine in its total essence without flaw, that I would do, not for a moment but for all eternity. Instead, I defer completely to Your saving grace, for within this frame of human frailty bears no ounce or fragment of perfection apart from the presence of Your indwelling Spirit. I submit my life as an offering poured out in a sweet discord of broken melodies. Though applause may come from those who observe or benefit from this *imperfect rhapsody* (*my life*), I long evermore to see You rise from the balcony in satisfaction with the life I've offered. Not of my own accord, but all this is from You, who reconciled me to You through Christ Jesus (2 Corinthians 5:18). Did I tell You I love You today? Did I tell You I miss You today? Did I tell You "thank You" today? Did I tell You that I "just want to be with You?" The end I seek is to give You all of me. It is the only reasonable response to the *ineffable sacrifice* you willingly gave on the cross (**Your life**). The relationship I desire is that of true love and allegiance to You; You are Love. The life I live is to become the best worshipper of You in this phase of existence as I ever hope to be in the phase called next, for eternity has already begun.

To my *cherished* **Flower**, words cannot adequately express the sincere appreciation I have for you and your impact on the trajectory of my life. I'm a better man, husband, dad, pharmacist, author, teacher, and preacher because of your faithfulness to our Savior. I look forward to changing the world with you! We will absolutely leave it better than we found it!

To my *sweet* **Makayela**, I love being your dad! You've taught me so much about gentleness, patience, and appreciating unique personalities. I love your hugs and can't wait for the next one. They teleport me to the fourth dimension and back faster than the speed of light! I admire your strength and it never ceases to amaze me how you bounce back so quickly from adversity and rejection. You're my hero in that regard. You maintain a sense of "you-ness" and you don't allow others to change who you are and I respect that greatly. God is going to do wonderful things through you because you know who you are and you know whose you are without compromise.

To my *darling* **Maddie**, the most affectionate, loving, and polite twelve-year-old I know. You bring a wonderful element of love to our five-pack! Thank you for never letting my need for affection run dry! I can always count on you to evoke a smile secondary to your words of kindness and affirmation. You are a fantastic artist and I can't wait to requisition your services for the illustration of the children's book series that has yet to be born.

To my *dearest* **Micah**, never more did I wish that you were able to comprehend the depth of this literary work. Nevertheless, I'm sure your advanced intelligence will find something relevant to talk about in your circle of influence. Thank you for reminding me that I'm special to God, Jesus, and the Holy Spirit. Thank you for audibly praying for the family before meals and at bedtime. Thank you for proving the scripture that Jesus has perfected praise from the mouths of babes. I've seen and heard you do more spiritual things than some people four times your age and I can't wait to see what God is going to do through you!

To my honored **Reader**, I pray that the pages you are about to read will intrigue and captivate you beyond your unexpected expectations. May you laugh, cry, pray, sing, dance, forgive, and seek the face and heart of the THE ONE who created yours.

Preface:

~~~~~~~~~~~~~~~~~~~~~~~~~~~~~~~~~~~~~~~

B orn from years of experience and a personal relationship with God, Destination **Heartland** provides daily scripture on which to meditate while also challenging readers to put the scripture into practice. Scriptures from different books of the Bible have been connected to express a truth and present a challenge to put it into action. Destination Heartland highlights the underlying truth that the entire Bible is inspired and God-breathed. The book consists of 183 devotionals in a daily scripture format accompanied by an application. The final 10 bonus devotionals are written in a manner that leaves the reader pondering, meditating, and wanting to pursue and praise God. Ruminate on one devotional, working to apply it over a couple of days, or go through them daily and cover each devotional twice in one year's time. Either approach permits the opportunity to plant 183 devotionals within the **"Land of the Heart"** in 365 days.

I have hidden your word in my heart that I might not sin against you. (Psalm 119:11 NIV)

183 devotionals to plant in 365 days

Introduction:

I am writing to you, my children, for your sins have been forgiven because of Christ's name. I am writing to you, fathers, because you know Him Who has been from the beginning. I am writing to you, young men, because you have power over the devil. I have written to you, young boys and girls, because you have learned to know the Father. I have written to you, fathers, because you know Him Who has been from the beginning. I have written to you, young men, because you are strong. You have kept God's Word in your hearts. You have power over the devil. (1 John 2:12-14 New Life Version).

Scripture for today (#1): Most certainly I tell you, unless a grain of wheat falls into the earth and dies, it remains by itself alone. But if it dies, it bears much fruit. He who loves his life will lose it. He who hates his life in this world will keep it to eternal life. (John 12:24-25 World English Bible).

Application for today: At Baptism, we died and became "new creatures" (2 Corinthians 5:17, Galatians 2:20). Today, let's allow the Holy Spirit to live "through" us. In doing so, we will be godly Christians who are intentional, wise, and nurturing. Also, when our patience becomes thin at work and at home we will realize that in our weakness, His Grace abounds and He will see us through. (2 Corinthians 12:9).

Scripture for today (#2): They said to each other, "Did not our hearts burn within us while He talked to us on the way and while He opened the Scriptures to us?" (Luke 24:32 MEV)

Application for today: Many people get excited about many different things. Let it be said of us today that we did not live by bread alone, but yearned for every word that God has spoken.

All Scripture is inspired by God and is useful to teach us what is true and to make us realize what is wrong in our lives. It corrects us when we are wrong and teaches us to do what is right. (2 Timothy 3:16 NLT).

Scripture for today (#3): I have told you these things, that in me you may have peace. In the world you have trouble; but cheer up! I have overcome the world. (John 16:33 WEB).

Application for today: Each day we are faced with challenges from many different angles. Remember, in Jesus, the battle is already won!

Scripture for today (#4): For we walk by faith and not by sight. (2 Corinthians 5:7 ESV).

Application for today: If you have to choose between your feelings and your faith. Always choose your faith!

Scripture for today (#5): And whatever you do or say, do it as a representative of the Lord Jesus, giving thanks through him to God the Father (Colossians 3:17 NLT)

Application for today: Whether it be fasting, service, prayer, or even going about your daily routine at work or at home, do everything cheerfully and with the motivation to honor God.

Scripture for today (#6): You will keep the mind that is dependent on you in perfect peace, for it is trusting in you. (Isaiah 26:3 CSB).

Application for today: We don't know what today holds, but we do know Who holds today! Keep your mind focused on Him and not the obstacles that come your way.

Scripture for today (#7): But you belong to God, my dear children. You have already won a victory over those people, because the Spirit who lives in you is greater than the spirit who lives in the world. (1 John 4:4 NLT).

Application for today: Whatever challenges or temptations Satan brings your way today, the Holy Spirit within you is Greater than our adversary. Trust in His strength to help you overcome.

Scripture for today (#8): Soldiers don't get tied up in the affairs of civilian life, for then they cannot please the officer who enlisted them. (2 Timothy 2:4 NLT).

Application for today: "Dear friends, I warn you as "temporary residents and foreigners" to keep away from worldly desires that wage war against your very souls." (1 Peter 2:11 NLT).

Scripture for today (#9): I no longer call you slaves, because a master doesn't confide in his slaves. Now you are my friends, since I have told you everything the Father told me. (John 15:15 NLT).

Application for today: In addition to Jesus being King of kings and Lord of lords, He's also your Friend. Let's make sure it's a "2-way" relationship and pray without ceasing. (1 Thessalonians 5:17 KJV).

Scripture for today (#10): The members of the council were amazed when they saw the boldness of Peter and John, for they could see that they were ordinary men with no special training in the Scriptures. They also recognized them as men who had been with Jesus. (Acts 4:13 NLT).

Application for today: Let it be said that you were mistaken for Jesus. May others recognize that you've been with Him!

Scripture for today (#11): He must become greater and greater, and I must become less and less. (John 3:30 NLT).

Application for today: Jesus continued to say to all of them, "Any of you who want to be my follower must stop thinking about yourself and what you want. You must be willing to carry the cross that is given to you every day for following me. (Luke 9:23 ERV).

Scripture for today (#12): Yet those who wait for the LORD Will gain new strength; They will mount up with wings like eagles, They will run and not get tired, They will walk and not become weary. (Isaiah 40:31 NASB).

Application for today: For we who worship by the Spirit of God are the ones who are truly circumcised. We rely on what Christ Jesus has done for us. We put no confidence in human effort. (Philippians 3:3 NLT).

Scripture for today (#13): Some trust in chariots and some in horses, but we trust in the name of the LORD our God (Psalm 20:7 NIV)

Application for today: We put our trust not in the created things, but in the ONE who created ALL things!

Scripture for today (#14): Consider it all joy, my brethren, when you encounter various trials, knowing that the testing of your faith produces endurance. And let endurance have its perfect result, so that you may be perfect and complete, lacking in nothing. (James 1:2-4 NASB).

Application for today: God allows trials to come into our lives to "make us", not to break us. He permits them to make us "better", not bitter. Let's take joy today in whatever may come our way!

Scripture for today (#15): You will keep in perfect peace all who trust in you, all whose thoughts are fixed on you! Trust in the Lord always, for the Lord God is the eternal Rock. (Isaiah 26:3-4 NLT).

Application for today: Many distractions await our attention today, let's make an intentional choice to fix our thoughts on the Lord and reap the reward of perfect peace.

Scripture for today (#16): Jesus answered, "I tell you the truth, before Abraham was even born, I Am !" (John 8:58 NLT).

Application for today: Jesus was, Jesus is, and Jesus always will be. He is from everlasting to everlasting. He is overqualified to handle our problems today!

Scripture for today (#17): And we know that all things work together for good for those who love God, for those who are called according to his purpose. (Romans 8:28 The Lexham English Bible).

Application for today: Individually, the circumstances of our lives may be extremely challenging, but the God of Heaven's armies is working it all together for our good. Let's greet the world with a smile today that proves that our God is an Awesome God!

Scripture for today (#18): Then, because so many people were coming and going that they did not even have a chance to eat, he said to them, "Come with me by yourselves to a quiet place and get some rest." (Mark 6:31 NIV).

Application for today: Take time to rest. Make time to rest. Get some rest.

Scripture for today (#19): It is the same with my word. I send it out, and it always produces fruit. It will accomplish all I want it to, and it will prosper everywhere I send it. (Isaiah 55:11 NLT).

Application for today: As we spend time in God's word daily, we discover the wonderful promises it contains. It's like mining for precious stones containing priceless jewels. His Word is truth.

Scripture for today (#20): I can do all things through Christ which strengtheneth me .(Philippians 4:13 KJV).

Application for today: This indeed is the secret of contentment. Whether today finds us abounding or lacking...let's remember where our help comes from.

Scripture for today (#21): For God has not given us a spirit of fearfulness, but one of power, love, and sound judgment. (2 Timothy 1:7 HCSB).

Application for today: Yielding to the power of the Holy Spirit gives us the boldness we need to step out in faith as we follow Jesus wherever he might lead.

Scripture for today (#22): Therefore, go and make disciples of all the nations, baptizing them in the name of the Father and the Son and the Holy Spirit. Teach these new disciples to obey all the commands I have given you. And be sure of this: I am with you always, even to the end of the age. (Matthew 28:19-20 NLT).

Application for today: We have our marching orders. Let us go forth in obedience and seek to please the One who has called us to this great work.

Scripture for today (#23): whether Paul or Apollos or Peter, or the world, or life and death, or the present and the future. Everything belongs to you, and you belong to Christ, and Christ belongs to God. (1 Corinthians 3:22-23 NLT).

Application for today: There is nothing we can ask God for that is greater than what He has already given us in Jesus Christ.—Demario L. Rollins

Scripture for today (#24): I am the Lord; that is my name; my glory I give to no other, nor my praise to carved idols. (Isaiah 42:8 ESV).

Application for today: As your good works attract the attention of others, channel all your praise and accomplishments toward Heaven. Give God the glory.

Scripture for today (#25): But without faith it is impossible to please him: for he that cometh to God must believe that he is, and that he is a rewarder of them that *diligently* seek him. (Hebrews 11:6 KJV)

Application for today: [1]*diligent* [dil-i-juhnt] 1. constant in effort to accomplish something; attentive and persistent in doing anything: 2. done or pursued with persevering attention

Have faith. Believe that He is. Seek Him diligently.

---

[1] Dictionary.com Online, s.v. "diligent," accessed August 20, 2020, https://www.dictionary.com/browse/diligent?s=t

Scripture for today (#26): For here we do not have a permanent city, but we seek the *city* that is to come. (Hebrews 13:14 Lexham English Bible).

Application for today: Therefore through him let us offer up a sacrifice of praise *continually* to God, that is, the fruit of lips that confess his name. (Hebrews 13:15 NIV).

Scripture for today (#27): So we don't look at the troubles we can see now; rather, we fix our gaze on things that cannot be seen. For the things we see now will soon be gone, but the things we cannot see will last forever. (2 Corinthians 4:18 NLT).

Application for today: Choose to live not according to what's going on around you but according to the joy that is within...given to you by Jesus Christ.

Scripture for today (#28): For our struggle is not against flesh and blood, but against the rulers, against the authorities, against the powers of this dark world and against the spiritual forces of evil in the heavenly realms. (Ephesians 6:12 NIV).

Application for today: We have one enemy. It is not our boss, spouse, kids, or government. Today, through prayer, let's make sure we're fighting the one true adversary who seeks our destruction, Satan.

Scripture for today (#29): Then the king called in the man he had forgiven and said, 'You evil servant! I forgave you that tremendous debt because you pleaded with me. Shouldn't you have mercy on your fellow servant, just as I had mercy on you?' (Matthew 18:32-33 NLT).

Application for today: Psalm 103:12 says "as far as the east is from the west, so far has he removed our transgressions from us." If He has forever severed our sins from our souls, most certainly we can forgive mankind for his/her offenses toward us today. Let's do it!

Scripture for today (#30): God cares for you, so turn all your worries over to him. (1 Peter 5:7 CEV).

Application for today: Decide today that you will defer the weight of the world to the One True God.

> *Learn to give more and more of your daily cares to the One who cares daily for you"*—Demario L. Rollins

Thought for today (#31): "If we could just see God as big as He really is, then perhaps we could perceive our problems to be as small as they really are."– Demario L. Rollins

Application for today: Whatever we focus on grows. May we shift our focus today off of our problems and cement a steady gaze upon the Glory and Majesty of The Most High.

Jude 24,25 (King James Version), Ephesians 3:20,21 (King James Version)

24 Now unto him that is able to keep you from falling, and to present you faultless before the presence of his glory with exceeding joy,
25 To the only wise God our Saviour, be glory and majesty, dominion and power, both now and ever. Amen.
20 Now unto him that is able to do exceeding abundantly above all that we ask or think, according to the power that worketh in us,
21 Unto him be glory in the church by Christ Jesus throughout all ages, world without end. Amen.

Scripture for today (#32): The spirit often throws him into the fire or into water, trying to kill him. Have mercy on us and help us, *if you can*." "What do you mean, 'If I can'?" Jesus asked. "Anything is possible if a person believes." The father instantly cried out, "I do believe, but help me overcome my unbelief!" (Mark 9:22-24 NLT).

Application for today: Let's shift the "if" today. The "if" does not belong in the realm of the uncontested Almighty Everlasting God. Rather, the "if" resides in our hearts as it relates to the capacity of our faith to believe in His unlimited ability. —Demario L. Rollins

Thought for today (#33): "Each day I am permitted to breathe, every decision I make, every word I speak, every action performed, every forgiveness granted, and every passing thought is filtered with and through this one question…."How do I want to be remembered?"—Demario L. Rollins

Application for today: Today is a page in the chapter of your life being written. God only knows when your book will come to an end. May the readers of your literary masterpiece comprehend from your performance today that you were a serious disciple of the blessed and only Potentate, the King of kings, and Lord of lords. (1 Timothy 6:15 KJV).;

Scripture for today (#34): If you do what is right, will you not be accepted? But if you do not do what is right, sin is crouching at your door; it desires to have you, but you must rule over it. (Genesis 4:7 NIV).

Application for today: Those who have been born into God's family do not make a practice of sinning, because God's life is in them. So they can't keep on sinning, because they are children of God. (1 John 3:9 NIV).

Scripture for today (#35): "I am the Lord, the God of all the peoples of the world. Is anything too hard for Me?(Jeremiah 32:27 NLT).

Application for today: But Jesus looked at them and said, "With man this is impossible, but with God all things are possible." (Matthew 19:26 ESV).

You may "face" an impossible situation today, turn 180 degrees and "face" the ONE who can do the impossible.

Scripture for today (#36): Do you not know? Have you not heard? The Lord is the everlasting God, the Creator of the whole earth. He never becomes faint or weary; there is no limit to his understanding. (Isaiah 40:28 CSB).

Application for today:[2]*omniscient* [om-nish-*uh*nt] 1. Having complete or unlimited knowledge, awareness, or understanding; perceiving all things.

Our God is omniscient! He knows absolutely everything; including...how to help us navigate through today. Trust in His infinite wisdom and yield to the guidance of the Holy Spirit

---

[2] Dictionary.com Online, s.v. "omniscient," accessed August 31, 2020, https://www.dictionary.com/browse/omniscient?s=t

Scripture for today (#37): Psalm 139:7-12 (New Living Translation)

7. I can never escape from your Spirit! I can never get away from your presence!
8. If I go up to heaven, you are there; if I go down to the grave, you are there.
9. If I ride the wings of the morning, if I dwell by the farthest oceans,
10. even there your hand will guide me, and your strength will support me.
11. I could ask the darkness to hide me and the light around me to become night—
12. but even in darkness I cannot hide from you. To you the night shines as bright as day.
Darkness and light are the same to you.

Application for today: [3]*omnipresent* [om-nuh-prez-uhnt] 1. Present everywhere at the same time
Our God is omnipresent! For in Him we live and move and exist (Acts 17:28a). We cannot escape His presence, henceforth, let us enjoy His presence incessantly!

---

[3] Dictionary.com Online, s.v. "omnipresent," accessed September 1 2020, https://www.dictionary.com/browse/omnipresent?s=t

Scripture for today (#38): "If we are thrown into the blazing furnace, the God whom we serve is able to save us. He will rescue us from your power, Your Majesty." (Daniel 3:17 NLT).

Application for today: [4]*omnipotent* [om-**nip**-*uh*-tu*h*nt] 1. almighty or infinite in power 2. Having very great or unlimited authority or power.

Our God is omnipotent! He can handle anything that comes our way today!

---

[4]   Dictionary.com Online, s.v. "omnipotent," accessed September 2, 2020,
https://www.dictionary.com/browse/omnipotent?s=t

Scripture for today (#39): "But even if he doesn't, we want to make it clear to you, your majesty, that we will never serve your gods or worship the gold statue you have set up."
(Daniel 3:18 NLT).

Application for today: God is able to do well beyond what our minds can conceive (Ephesians 3:20), but _sometimes He chooses not_ to answer our prayers exactly as we desire. In those times of confusion, doubt, and disappointment we must maintain our commitment not to bow to the Enemy.

Scripture for today (#40): When Jesus had tasted it, he said, "It is finished!" Then he bowed his head and released his spirit. (John 19:30 NLT).

Application for today: As we battle Satan today, remember, we are not fighting "for" the position of victory but "from" a position of victory.

Scripture for today (#41): If only there were a mediator between us, someone who could bring us together. (Job 9:33 NLT).

Application for today: Praise God that 1 Timothy 2:5 answers Job's plea. "For, There is one God and one Mediator who can reconcile God and humanity—the man Christ Jesus." (NLT).

We can face a hostile world today because we have peace with God through Jesus Christ.

Scripture for today (#42): You didn't choose me. I chose you. (John15:16a NLT).

Application for today: You are important. You are special. You are necessary. You are not an accident. Almighty God chose you!

Scripture for today (#43): For I am confident of this very thing, that He who began a good work in you will perfect it until the day of Christ Jesus. (Philippians 1:6 NASB).

Application for today: Today you may feel like you have an "Under Construction" sign on the billboard of your life. You're not alone. We are all "works in progress" and Jesus will continue His work until He calls us home. He's not finished with you yet!

Scripture for today (#44): So then, my dear brothers, be steadfast, immovable, always abounding in the work of the Lord, *because you* know that your labor is not *in* vain in the Lord. (1 Corinthians 15:58 LEB).

Application for today: Many of the sacrifices we make and the hardships we endure can seem to go unnoticed by those around us. Rest assured, Jesus says *"if you give even a cup of cold water to one of the least of my followers, you will surely be rewarded"* (Matthew 10:42 NLT). Never give up!

Scripture for today (#45): However, each man among you [without exception] is to love his wife as his very own self [with behavior worthy of respect and esteem, always seeking the best for her with an attitude of lovingkindness], and the wife [must see to it] that she respects *and* delights in her husband [that she notices him and prefers him and treats him with loving concern, treasuring him, honoring him, and holding him dear]. (Ephesians 5:33 Amplified Bible).

Application for today: "Try to enjoy every day with your significant other as if it's the last. Tomorrow isn't promised to any of us. All that we have today could be gone tomorrow, including our lives. Think before you speak, say only what you wouldn't mind being repeated on the loudspeaker at a Major League Baseball game. Smile, laugh, and savor special moments. Carve special memories in stone and remember them forever. Write your hurts on the seaside so that the tide will wash their memory away."— *Demario L. Rollins*

Scripture for today (#46): For it is by grace [God's remarkable compassion and favor drawing you to Christ] that you have been saved [actually delivered from judgment and given eternal life] through faith. And this [salvation] is not of yourselves [not through your own effort], but it is the [undeserved, gracious] gift of God; not as a result of [your] works [nor your attempts to keep the Law], so that no one will [be able to] boast or take credit in any way [for his salvation]. (Ephesians 2:8-9 Amplified Bible).

Application for today: "There's NOTHING we can do to earn 1 second in Heaven, even on our best day, BUT because of EVERYTHING He has done we get to spend Eternity there, that is Amazing grace."—Demario L. Rollins

Scripture for today (#47): For everyone born of God is victorious *and* overcomes the world; and this is the victory that has conquered *and* overcome the world—our [continuing, persistent] faith [in Jesus the Son of God]. (1 John 5:4 Amplified Bible).

Application for today: "There is no circumstance that you see with your eyes that can't be dissolved by the knowledge of your faith"—Demario L. Rollins

Scripture for today (#48): For the time being no discipline brings joy, but seems sad *and* painful; yet to those who have been trained by it, afterwards it yields the peaceful fruit of righteousness [right standing with God and a lifestyle and attitude that seeks conformity to God's will and purpose]. (Hebrews 12:11 Amplified Bible).

Application for today: My dear child, don't shrug off God's discipline, but don't be crushed by it either. It's the child he loves that he disciplines; the child he embraces, he also corrects. God is educating you; that's why you must never drop out. He's treating you as dear children. This trouble you're in isn't punishment; it's *training*, the normal experience of children. (Hebrews 12:5-7 The Message).

Scripture for today (#49): Though the cherry trees don't blossom and the strawberries don't ripen, Though the apples are worm-eaten and the wheat fields stunted, Though the sheep pens are sheepless and the cattle barns empty, I'm singing joyful praise to God. I'm turning cartwheels of joy to my Savior God. Counting on God's Rule to prevail, I take heart and gain strength. I run like a deer. I feel like I'm king of the mountain! (Habakkuk 3:17-19 The Message).

Application for today: When everything around us seems like it's going wrong, He is still worthy of our praise!

> Why, my soul, are you downcast? Why so disturbed within me?
>
> Put your hope in God, for I will yet praise him, my Savior and my God. (Psalm 42:11 NIV).

Scriptures for today (#50):

> ***Jeremiah 31:34b (NLT):*** "And I will for-give their wickedness, and I will never again remember their sins."

> ***Hebrews 8:12b (NLT):*** "And I will for-give their wickedness, and I will never again remember their sins."

> ***Hebrews 10:17b (NLT):*** "I will never again remember their sins and law-less deeds."

Application for today: When a teacher "purposely" repeats something in school, it will most likely be on the test. When God repeats something 3 times, He must REALLY mean it!

Then Jesus stood up again and said to the woman, "Where are your accusers? Didn't even one of them condemn you?" "No, Lord," she said. And Jesus said, "**Neither do I. Go and sin no more.**" (John 8:10-11 NLT).

Scripture for today (#51): If you need wisdom, ask our generous God, and he will give it to you. He will not rebuke you for asking. (James 1:5 NLT).

Application for today: But when you ask him, *be sure that your faith is in God alone.* Do not waver, for a person with divided loyalty is as unsettled as a wave of the sea that is blown and tossed by the wind. (James 1:6 NLT).

Scripture for today (#52): When I fed them, they were satisfied; when they were satisfied, they became proud; then they forgot me. (Hosea 13:6 NIV).

Application for today: O God, I beg two favors from you; let me have them before I die. First, help me never to tell a lie. Second, give me neither poverty nor riches! Give me just enough to satisfy my needs. For if I grow rich, I may deny you and say, "Who is the Lord?" And if I am too poor, I may steal and thus insult God's holy name. (Proverbs 30:7-9 NLT).

Scripture for today (#53): Don't cause the Holy Spirit sorrow by the way you live. Remember, he is the one who marks you to be present on that day when salvation from sin will be complete. (Ephesians 4:30 The Living Bible).

Application for today: Instead, be kind and compassionate to one another, forgiving one another, just as God in Christ has forgiven us. (Ephesians 4:32 Evangelical Heritage Version).

Scripture for today (#54): Jesus got up early in the morning, while it was still dark, and went out. He withdrew to a solitary place and was praying there. (Mark 1:35 EHV).

Application for today: Purpose to get alone with the Master today and every day. Seek Him early. Some would say, "I'm too busy to pray!" We say, "I'm too busy not to pray!"

> *...and those that seek me early shall find me.*
> (Proverbs 8:17b KJV).

Scripture for today (#55): No temptation has over-taken you that is unusual for human beings. But God is faithful, and he will not allow you to be tempted beyond your strength. Instead, along with the temp-tation he will also provide a way out, so that you may be able to endure it. (1 Corinthians 10:13 ISV).

Application for today: Temptations are sure to come today. Look for the EXIT door! Jesus promised to create one.

> And he said to his disciples,
> "Temptations to sin are sure to come,
> but woe to the one through whom
> they come! (Luke 17:1 ESV).

Scripture for today (#56): Jesus said to him, "Because you have seen Me, do you now believe? Blessed [happy, spiritually secure, and favored by God] are they who did not see [Me] and yet believed [in Me]." (John 20:29 Amplified Bible).

Application for today: Do you believe in Jesus Christ as your Lord and Savior without having seen Him with your eyes?

You are happy.
　　　　　You are spiritually secure.
　　　　　　　　　You are favored by God.
　　　　　　　　　　You are Blessed.

Scripture for today (#57): Though you have not seen him, you love him; and even though you do not see him now, you believe in him and are filled with an inexpressible and glorious joy. (1 Peter 1:8 NIV).

Application for today: Hold tight to what you believe, today and every day. No matter how tough it gets, never forsake the GOSPEL, *"for you are receiving the end result of your faith, the salvation of your souls"*. (1 Peter 1:9 NIV).

Scripture for today (#58): Imitate God, therefore, in everything you do, because you are his dear children. (Ephesians 5:1 NLT).

Application for today: [5]*imitate* [**im**-i-teyt] 1. to follow or endeavor to follow as a model or example: 2. to mimic; impersonate: 3. to have or assume the appearance of; simulate; resemble.

The one who claims to remain in him ought to live in the same way as he lived. (1 John 2:6 CEB).

---

[5] Dictionary.com Online, s.v. "imitate," accessed September 22, 2020, https://www.dictionary.com/browse/imitate?s=t

Scripture for today (#59): For our citizenship is in heaven, from which we also eagerly wait for the Savior, the Lord Jesus Christ. (Philippians 3:20 NKJV).

[6]Citizenship [**sit**-*uh*-zuhn-ship]: the state of being vested with the rights, privileges, and duties of a citizen.
[7]Citizen [**sit**-*uh*-zuhn: a native or naturalized member of a state or nation who owes allegiance to its government and is entitled to its protection.

Application for today: But the day of the Lord will come as unexpectedly as a thief. Then the heavens will pass away with a terrible noise, and the very elements themselves will disappear in fire, and the earth and everything on it will be found to deserve judgment. Since everything around us is going to be destroyed like this, what holy and godly lives you should live. (2 Peter 3:10 NLT).

---

[6]   Dictionary.com Online, s.v. "citizenship," accessed September 23, 2020, https://www.dictionary.com/browse/citizenship?s=t

[7]   Dictionary.com Online, s.v. "citizen," accessed September 23, 2020, https://www.dictionary.com/browse/citizen?s=t

Scripture for today (#60): "Don't store up treasures here on earth, where moths eat them and rust destroys them, and where thieves break in and steal". (Matthew 6:19 NLT).

Application for today: Store your treasures in heaven, where moths and rust cannot destroy, and thieves do not break in and steal. Wherever your treasure is, there the desires of your heart will also be. (Matthew 6:20-21 NLT).

Scripture for today (#61): Praise be to the God and Father of our Lord Jesus Christ, who has blessed us in the heavenly realms with every spiritual blessing in Christ. (Ephesians 1:3 NIV).

Application for today: With the amazing gift of eyesight it is relatively easy to notice what we lack in this life. With the precious gift of faith, may we accept and believe that our Heavenly Father has already (past tense) blessed us in the heavenly realms with every spiritual blessing in Christ.

He who did not spare his own Son, but gave him up for us all—how will he not also, along with him, graciously give us all things? (Romans 8:32 NIV).

Scripture for today (#62): just as [in His love] He chose us in Christ [actually selected us for Himself as His own] before the foundation of the world, so that we would be holy [that is, consecrated, set apart for Him, purpose-driven] and blameless in His sight. In love. (Ephesians 1:4 Amplified Bible).

Application for today: "You mean to tell me that I was on God's mind and heart before He created Adam and He had a redemption plan in place before I needed one? Yes! Amen! Selah!

And **you** (dear reader) were on His mind too!

> This is love: not that we loved God, but that he loved us and sent his Son as an atoning sacrifice for our sins. (1 John 4:10 NIV).

Scripture for today (#63): God destined us to be his adopted children through Jesus Christ because of his love. This was according to his goodwill and plan. (Ephesians 1:5 CEB).

Application for today: You may be confused, puzzled, worried, perplexed and anxious about the future. Read very carefully...God consistently, repeatedly, continuously, perpetually, invariably, and always has a **plan**!

Your eyes saw me when I was still an unborn child. Every day of my life was recorded in your book before one of them had taken place. (Psalm 139:16 God's Word Translation).

Go ahead and make all the plans you want, but it's the Lord who will ultimately direct your steps. (Proverbs 16:1 The Passion Translation).

Scriptures for today (#64): It was just before the Passover Festival. Jesus knew that the hour had come for him to leave this world and go to the Father. Having loved his own who were in the world, *he loved them to the end*. (John 13:1 NIV).

> And as for me, I will most gladly *spend everything* I have *and be spent myself* too for your sakes. (2 Corinthians 12:15 Complete Jewish Bible).

Application for today: Totally commit to sacrificing everything for your **_spouse_**, **_children_**, **_family_**, and **_neighbor_**. When the body you've been given ceases to exchange oxygen for carbon dioxide, let it be said of you that there was nothing left to give (having given it all to make the world and those around you better because of your unconditional love).

Husbands, go all out in your love for your **_wives_**, exactly as Christ did for the church—a love marked by giving, not getting. Christ's love makes the church whole. His words evoke her beauty. Everything he does and says is designed to bring the best out of her, dressing her in dazzling white silk, radiant with holiness. And that is how husbands ought to love their wives. They're really doing themselves a favor—since they're already "one" in marriage. (Ephesians 5:25-28 MSG).

and the wife [must see to it] that she respects *and* delights in her **husband** [that she notices him and prefers him and treats him with loving concern, treasuring him, honoring him, and holding him dear]. (Ephesians 5:33b Amplified Bible).

Fathers [or Parents; Heb. 11:23], do not ·nag [aggravate; exasperate; provoke] your **children** [Eph. 6:4]. If you are too hard to please, they may want to stop trying [become discouraged; lose heart]. (Colossians 3:21 The Expanded Bible).

> The second is equally important: 'Love your **neighbor** as yourself.' No other commandment is greater than these." (Mark 12:31 NLT).

Whoever does not care for his own relatives, especially his own **family** members, has turned against [denied; rejected] the faith and is worse than someone who does not believe in God [an unbeliever]. (1 Timothy 5:8 The Expanded Bible).

(Note: **bold**, *italics* and underline added for emphasis)

Scriptures for today (#65): Humans can reproduce only human life, but the Holy Spirit gives birth to spiritual life. So don't be surprised when I say, 'You must be born again.' (John 3:6-7 NLT). The wind blows where it wishes and you hear its sound, but you do not know where it is coming from and where it is going; so it is with everyone who is born of the Spirit. (John 3:8 AMP).

Application for today: Spiritual birth is an intangible process performed from start to finish by the Trinity. Let's be careful *"not to judge"* (in a condemning way) whether this miraculous experience has or has not occurred in someone else's life. The conversion process is precious and personal between each created soul and the Creator. If we have doubts about someone else's salvation, we should encourage and pray for that individual daily and "expect" to see positive fruit in their life.—Demario L. Rollins

Scripture for today (#66): When you are invited to a wedding feast, don't sit in the seat of honor. What if someone who is more distinguished than you has also been invited? The host will come and say, 'Give this person your seat.' Then you will be embarrassed, and you will have to take whatever seat is left at the foot of the table! (Luke 14:8-9 NLT).

Application for today: "Instead, take the lowest place at the foot of the table. Then when your host sees you, he will come and say, 'Friend, we have a better place for you!' Then you will be honored in front of all the other guests. (Luke 14:10 NLT).

> So humble yourselves under the mighty power of God, and at the right time he will lift you up in honor. (1 Peter 5:6 NLT).

Scripture for today (#67): All Scripture is inspired by God and is useful to teach us what is true and to make us realize what is wrong in our lives. It corrects us when we are wrong and teaches us to do what is right. God uses it to prepare and equip his people to do every good work. (2 Timothy 3:16 NLT).

Application for today: Action steps created from rephrasing Psalm 119:10-16 NLT

10 Try hard to find Him—pray that He doesn't let you wander from His commands
11 Hide His word in your heart so that you won't sin against Him
12 Praise Him, ask Him to teach you His decrees
13 Recite His regulations aloud
14 Rejoice in His laws as much as in riches
15 Study His commandments and reflect on His ways
16 Delight in His decrees and do not forget His word

Scriptures for today (#68):

And the man said to me, "Daniel, **you are very precious to God**, so listen carefully to what I have to say to you (Daniel 10:11a NLT).

"Don't be afraid," he said, "**for you are very precious to God**. Peace! Be encouraged! Be strong!" As he spoke these words to me, I suddenly felt stronger and said to him, "Please speak to me, my lord, for you have strengthened me." (Daniel 10:19 NLT).

For **God does not show favoritism**. (Romans 2:11 NLT)

Then Peter replied, "I see very clearly that **God shows no favoritism**. (Acts 10:34 NLT)

Application for today: Daniel 10:19 + Romans 2:11 = **You** are very precious to God!

(Note: **bold** and *italics* added for emphasis)

Scriptures for today (#69):

Daniel 4:30-31 As he looked out across the city, he said, 'Look at this great city of Babylon! *By my own mighty power, I have built this beautiful* city as my royal residence to display my majestic splendor.' "While these words were still in his mouth, a voice called down from heaven, 'O King Nebuchadnezzar, this message is for you! You are no longer ruler of this kingdom. (NLT).

Acts 12:21-23 and an appointment with Herod was granted. When the day arrived, Herod put on his royal robes, sat on his throne, and made a speech to them. The people gave him a great ovation, shouting, "It's the voice of a god, not of a man!" Instantly, an angel of the Lord struck Herod with a sickness, *because he accepted the people's worship instead of giving the glory to God*. So he was consumed with worms and died. (NLT).

Application for today: God opposes the proud but gives grace to the humble. Give glory to God today!

(Note: *italics* added for emphasis)

Scripture for today (#70): *We can rejoice,* too, when we run into problems and trials, for *we know* that they help us develop endurance. And endurance develops strength of character, and character strengthens our confident hope of salvation. (Romans 5:3-4 NLT).

Application for today: Problems are inevitable. They are expected visitors in a fallen world. However, because of what *we know, we can rejoice!* Live today according to what you know to be true and not according to the fallacies presented by your problems. There is a "process behind the problem".—Demario L. Rollins

Scripture for today (#71): "Do you think that I like to see wicked people die? says the Sovereign Lord. Of course not! I want them to turn from their wicked ways and live. (Ezekial 18:23 NLT).

Application for today: As we pursue the heart of God, we should come to desire what He desires. God does not want to see wicked people die and neither should we. Let's share the Gospel today. Earth desperately needs a savior!

Scripture for today (#72): But first *and* most importantly seek (aim at, strive after) His kingdom and His righteousness [His way of doing and being right— the attitude and character of God], and all these things will be given to you also. (Matthew 6:33 Amplified Bible).

Application for today: Put God first today in everything you do. Many distractions will compete with our focus on God and His righteousness. Therefore, make a *declaration* before today's *preparation* that you will honor God by having no other god(s) before Him.

Scripture for today (#73): "God blesses you when people mock you and persecute you and lie about you and say all sorts of evil things against you because you are my followers." (Matthew 5:11 NLT).

Application for today: Be happy about it! Be very glad! For a great reward awaits you in heaven. And remember, the ancient prophets were persecuted in the same way. (Matthew 5:12 NLT).

Scripture for today (#74): When they heard Paul speak about the resurrection of the dead, some laughed in contempt, but others said, "We want to hear more about this later." That ended Paul's discussion with them, *but some joined him* and became believers. Among them were Dionysius, a member of the council, a woman named Damaris, and others with them. (Acts 17:32-34 NLT).

Application for today: God has commissioned us to share the Good News as a way of life. It can be challenging because some people will laugh at us in contempt and others will dismiss us until a later time. BUT...*some will join us*! Share the Gospel today and see what happens!

Scriptures for today (#75): Should the thing that was created say to the one who created it, "Why have you made me like this?" (Romans 9:20b NLT).

You are confused. You think the clay is equal to the potter. You think that an object can tell the person who made it, "You didn't make me." This is like a pot telling its maker, "You don't know anything." (Isaiah 29:16 ICB).

Application for today: God does not make mistakes. He made *"you"* just the way *"He"* wanted to. Trust that "you" are acceptable to "Him" even if the world rejects you. Don't change who "you" are to satisfy humans who did not create you.

Scripture for today (#76): We have sufferings now. But the sufferings we have now are nothing compared to the great glory that will be given to us. (Romans 8:18 ICB).

Application for today: The weight of this world can be overbearing at times. Know today that you will be overcompensated in the world to come for the troubles of this present age.

He will wipe away every tear from their eyes, and death will not exist any more—or mourning, or crying, or pain, for the former things have ceased to exist." (Revelation 21:4 New English Translation).

Scripture for today (#77): Don't you realize how patient he is being with you? Or don't you care? Can't you see that he has been waiting all this time without punishing you, to give you time to turn from your sin? His kindness is meant to lead you to repentance. (Romans 2:4 TLB).

Application for today: God knows everything about us, yet He continues to pursue a relationship with us. Let us strip off every weight that slows us down, especially the sin that so easily trips us up. And let us renounce everything that brings shame to the Great Name that saved us!

In other words, God was reconciling the world to Himself through Christ, by not counting people's sins against them. He has trusted us with this message of reconciliation. (2 Corinthians 5:19 CEB).

Scriptures for today (#78): But anyone who believes that something he wants to do is wrong shouldn't do it. He sins if he does, for he thinks it is wrong, and so for him it *is* wrong. Anything that is done apart from what he feels is right is sin. (Romans 14:23 TLB).

Remember, too, that knowing what is right to do and then not doing it is sin. (James 4:17 TLB).

Application for today: Never damp the fire of the Spirit, and never despise what is spoken in the name of the Lord. By all means use your judgement, and hold on to whatever is really good, Steer clear of evil in any form. (1 Thessalonians 5:19-22 J.B. Phillips New Testament).

Scriptures for today (#79): It wasn't offerings and sacrifices I wanted from your fathers when I led them out of Egypt. That was not the point of my command. But what I told them was: *Obey* me, and I will be your God and you shall be my people; only do as I say, and all shall be well! (Jeremiah 7:22-23 TLB).

But Samuel replied, "What is more pleasing to the Lord: your burnt offerings and sacrifices or your obedience to his voice? Listen! Obedience is better than sacrifice, and submission is better than offering the fat of rams. (1 Samuel 15:22 NLT).

Application for today: "If you [really] love Me, you will keep *and* obey My commandments. (John 14:15 Amplified Bible) —Jesus Christ

Scripture for today (#80): Don't be misled: No one makes a fool of God. What a person plants, he will harvest. The person who plants selfishness, ignoring the needs of others—ignoring God!—harvests a crop of weeds. All he'll have to show for his life is weeds! But the one who plants in response to God, letting God's Spirit do the growth work in him, harvests a crop of real life, eternal life. (Galatians 6:7-8 The Message).

Application for today: So let's not allow ourselves to get fatigued doing good. At the right time we will harvest a good crop if we don't give up, or quit. Right now, therefore, every time we get the chance, let us work for the benefit of all, starting with the people closest to us in the community of faith. (Galatians 6:9-10 The Message).

Scripture for today (#81): Do not let unwholesome [foul, profane, worthless, vulgar] words ever come out of your mouth, but only such *speech* as is good for building up others, according to the need *and* the occasion, so that it will be a blessing to those who hear [you speak]. (Ephesians 4:29 Amplified Bible).

Application for today: Words satisfy the mind as much as fruit does the stomach; good talk is as gratifying as a good harvest. Words kill, words give life; they're either poison or fruit—you choose. (Proverbs 18:20-21 The Message).

Scripture for today (#82): You were once darkness, but now you are light in the Lord, so live your life as children of light. (Ephesians 5:8 CEB).

Application for today: If someone claims, "I know him well!" but doesn't keep his commandments, he's obviously a liar. His life doesn't match his words. But the one who keeps God's word is the person in whom we see God's mature love. This is the only way to be sure we're in God. Anyone who claims to be intimate with God ought to live the same kind of life Jesus lived. (1 John 2:4-6 The Message).

Scripture for today (#83): For it has been granted to you on behalf of Christ not only to believe in him, but also to suffer for him (Philippians 1:29 NIV).

Application for today: Dear friends, don't be bewildered or surprised when you go through the fiery trials ahead, for this is no strange, unusual thing that is going to happen to you. Instead, be really glad—because these trials will make you partners with Christ in his suffering, and afterwards you will have the wonderful joy of sharing his glory in that coming day when it will be displayed. (1 Peter 4:12-13 TLB).

Scripture for today (#84): Everything was created by him, everything in heaven and on earth, everything seen and unseen, including all forces and powers, and all rulers and authorities. All things were created by God's Son, and everything was made for him. (Colossians 1:16 CEV).

Application for today: We were made by Him and for Him. Therefore...

Let the words of my mouth, and the meditation of my heart, be acceptable in thy sight, O Lord, my strength, and my redeemer. (Psalm 19:14 KJV).

Scripture for today (#85): We are not saying that we can do this work ourselves. It is God who makes us able to do all that we do. (2 Corinthians 3:5 NCV).

Application for today: "I am the vine. You are the branches. If you remain joined to me, and I to you, you will bear a lot of fruit. You can't do anything without me." — Jesus (John 15:5 NIRV).

Scripture for today (#86): Put your heart and soul into every activity you do, as though you are doing it for the Lord himself and not merely for others. (Colossians 3:23 The Passion Translation).

Application for today: Remember that you will receive your reward from the Lord, which he promised to his people. You are serving the Lord Christ. (Colossians 3:24 NCV).

Scripture for today (#87): But godliness *actually* is a source of great gain when accompanied by contentment [that contentment which comes from a sense of inner confidence based on the sufficiency of God]. (1 Timothy 6:6 The Amplified Bible).

Application for today: For we have brought nothing into the world, so we cannot take anything out of it either. If we have food and covering, with these we shall be content. (1 Timothy 6:7-8 NASB).

Scripture for today (#88): "Lord, if it's you," Peter replied, "tell me to come to you on the water." "Come," he said. Then Peter got down out of the boat, walked on the water and came toward Jesus. But when he saw the wind, he was afraid and, beginning to sink, cried out, "Lord, save me!" (Matthew 14:28-30 NIV).

Application for today: Focusing on the storms of this world will *evoke* fear and failure. Fixing our eyes on Jesus will *invoke* the power of the Holy Spirit to do the incredible for His Kingdom and for His Glory. — Demario L. Rollins

Scripture for today (#89): Jesus called them together and said, "You know that the rulers of the Gentiles lord it over them, and their high officials exercise authority over them. Not so with you. Instead, whoever wants to become great among you must be your servant, and whoever wants to be first must be your slave. (Matthew 20:25-27 NIV).

Application for today: <u>Be like the Son of Man</u>. He did not come to be served. Instead, he came to serve others. He came to give his life as the price for setting many people free."

(Matthew 20:28 NIRV).

> *"Follow my example, just as I follow the example of Christ."* — Paul (1 Corinthians 11:1 ERV).

Scriptures for today (#90): **Delight** yourself in the Lord; And He will give you the desires of your heart. (Psalm 37:4 NASB).

If you **remain** in Me and My words remain in you [that is, if we are vitally **united** and My message lives in your heart], ask whatever you wish and it will be done for you. (John 15:7 Amplified Bible).

Application for today: Don't become like the people of this world. Instead, **change** the way you think. Then you will always be able to **determine** what God really wants—what is good, pleasing, and perfect. (Romans 12:2 Names of God Bible).

Delight...Remain...Unite...Change...Determine... ASK whatever you wish (which will then fall in line with God's wishes) and it will be done for you. Essentially, when you are conformed to the image of Christ through His Word, you begin to desire what God desires and will only pray for that which He already wills.
(Note: **bold** print added for emphasis)

Scripture for today (#91): Then he went into Jericho and was making his way through it. And here we find a wealthy man called Zacchaeus, a chief collector of taxes, wanting to see what sort of person Jesus was. But the crowd prevented him from doing so, for he was very short. So he ran ahead and climbed up into a sycamore tree to get a view of Jesus as he was heading that way. When Jesus reached the spot, he looked up and saw the man and said, "Zacchaeus, hurry up and come down. I must be your guest today." (Luke 19:1-5 J.B. Phillips New Testament).

Application for today: Zacchaeus had a DESIRE to see Jesus but had a DILEMMA in his stature. Nevertheless, he was DETERMINED and progressed to his DESTINY of eventual DELIVERANCE from the bondage of sin. Let's follow his example and move faithfully from "Desire" to "Deliverance".— Demario L. Rollins

Scripture for today (#92): Sanballat, Tobiah, Geshem the Arab, and the rest of our enemies found out that I had finished rebuilding the wall and that no gaps remained—though we had not yet set up the doors in the gates. So Sanballat and Geshem sent a message asking me to meet them at one of the villages in the plain of Ono. But I realized they were plotting to harm me, so I replied by sending this message to them: "I am engaged in a great work, so I can't come. Why should I stop working to come and meet with you?" (Nehemiah 6:1-3 NLT).

Application for today: As we continue the work of building and advancing God's Kingdom, there will always be Sanballats, Tobiahs, and Geshems. They will try to intimidate us into quitting. They will think to themselves, "They'll give up; they'll never finish the work God has for them." In response to these attempts to thwart our efforts, we will pray! We will not abandon the work!

They were trying to intimidate us into quitting. They thought, "They'll give up; they'll never finish it." I prayed, "Give me strength." (Nehemiah 6:9 The Message).

Scripture for today (#93): A man has joy in giving an appropriate answer, And how good *and* delightful is a word spoken at the right moment—how good it is! (Proverbs 15:23 Amplified Bible).

Application for today: Take time to "think" about what you want to say before it exits your mouth as "speech".

"You can be sure that on the Judgment Day you will have to give account of every useless word you have ever spoken". (Matthew 12:36 GNT).

Scripture for today (#94): He said: "Listen, King Jehoshaphat and all who live in Judah and Jerusalem! This is what the Lord says to you: 'Do not be afraid or discouraged because of this vast army. For the battle is not yours, but God's. (2 Chronicles 20:15 NIV).

Application for today: Be sober [well balanced and self-disciplined], be alert *and* cautious at all times. That enemy of yours, the devil, prowls around like a roaring lion [fiercely hungry], seeking someone to devour. (1 Peter 5:8 Amplified Bible).

Dear child of the Most High, your adversary and his fallen angels have assembled as a vast army. This is what the Lord says to you: 'Do not be afraid or discouraged because of this vast army. For the battle is not yours, but God's.

Scripture for today (#95): Carry one another's burdens, and in this way you will fulfill the law of Christ. (Galatians 6:2 New English Translation).

Application for today:

1. Take the time _today_ to genuinely ask someone else how they are doing.
2. Listen.
3. Really listen.
4. Don't interrupt.
5. Pray with them.
6. Look them in the eyes.
7. Tell them they are not alone.
8. Commit to help carry their burden.
9. and in this way you will fulfill the law of Christ. (Galatians 6:2).

Scripture for today (#96): Don't have anything to do with godless stories and silly tales (1 Timothy 4:7a NIRV).

Application for today: Instead, train yourself to be godly. "Physical training is good, but training for godliness is much better, promising benefits in this life and in the life to come." (1 Timothy 4:7b-8 NLT).

Scripture for today (#97): After this I saw a vast crowd, too great to count, from every nation and tribe and people and language, standing in front of the throne and before the Lamb. They were clothed in white robes and held palm branches in their hands. (Revelation 7:9 NLT).

Application for today: Take time today to be inclusive of all people groups. Smile at someone whose skin differs in pigment than yours. Open the door for someone whose hair has a different texture than yours. Offer to pray for someone whose palms differ in complexion than yours. In Heaven, there will be people from every nation and tribe and language. Let us make the sphere of influence we have look like Heaven.

Scripture for today (#98): "Yes, I am the vine; you are the branches. Those who *remain* in me, and I in them, will produce much fruit. For apart from me you can do nothing. (John 15:5 NLT).

Application for today: [8]*remain* [ri-meyn]: to continue in the same state

Keep praying, keep reading, keep listening, keep serving, keep believing, keep repenting.

Remain in Him and allow Him to remain in you. For apart from Him, you can do nothing!

---

[8] Dictionary.com Online, s.v. "remain," accessed November 1, 2020, https://www.dictionary.com/browse/remain?s=t

Scripture for today (#99): However, when ambassadors arrived from Babylon to ask about the remarkable events that had taken place in the land, God withdrew from Hezekiah in order to test him and to see what was really in his heart. (2 Chronicles 32:31 NLT).

Application for today: Your word I have hidden in my heart, that I might not sin against You (Psalm 119:11 Modern English Version).

Many times in our lives the voice of God can sound like the words between the book of Malachi and Matthew… silent, obsolete, missing, absent. The truth is, even if God remained silent until Christ's return, He's already said enough! Hide the Word in your heart and sin will surely be served an eviction notice.— Demario L. Rollins

Scriptures for today (#100): Now when the time was approaching for Him to be taken up [to heaven], He was *determined to go* to Jerusalem [to fulfill His purpose]. (Luke 9:51 Amplified Bible).

Jesus went through the towns and villages, teaching as he went, *always pressing on toward* Jerusalem. (Luke 13:22 NLT).

Application for today: With every footstep of His life, Jesus journeyed toward Jerusalem. He always had us in mind. We were His purpose. Today, reciprocate His love by letting your footsteps lead you to the Heavenly Jerusalem. Always have Him in mind. Make Him your purpose.

Scripture for today (#101): First, you must understand this: No prophecy in Scripture is a matter of one's own interpretation. No prophecy ever originated from humans. Instead, it was given by the Holy Spirit as humans spoke under God's direction. (2 Peter 1:20-21 Names of God Bible).

Application for today: Read your Bible aloud today. You are "literally" listening to the Words of the Most High God. What a privilege! What an experience! What a wonderful day!

Scripture for today (#102): One day Jesus said to his disciples, "Let's cross to the other side of the lake." So they got into a boat and started out. As they sailed across, Jesus settled down for a nap. But soon a fierce storm came down on the lake. The boat was filling with water, and they were in real danger. The disciples went and woke him up, shouting, "Master, Master, we're going to drown!" When Jesus woke up, he rebuked the wind and the raging waves. Suddenly the storm stopped and all was calm. Then he asked them, "Where is your faith?" The disciples were terrified and amazed. "Who is this man?" they asked each other. "When he gives a command, even the wind and waves obey him!" (Luke 8:22-25 NLT).

Application for today: You "will" cross to the other side of the "lake" you are traversing today. This too shall pass.

Scripture for today (#103): I want you to show love, not offer sacrifices. I want you to know me more than I want burnt offerings. (Hosea 6:6 NLT).

Application for today: Almighty God has told us what He wants. Let us go forth today showing love and getting to know Him through His word. Never let the gifts we give Him (sacrifices) substitute for the greater desire of His heart. He wants a relationship with us!

Scripture for today (#104): We are human, but we don't wage war as humans do. (2 Corinthians 10:3 NLT).

Application for today: We use God's mighty weapons, not worldly weapons, to knock down the strongholds of human reasoning and to destroy false arguments. We destroy every proud obstacle that keeps people from knowing God. We capture their rebellious thoughts and teach them to obey Christ. (2 Corinthians 10:4-5 NLT).

Scripture for today (#105): I have swept away your sins like a cloud. I have scattered your offenses like the morning mist. Oh, return to me, for I have paid the price to set you free." (Isaiah 44:22 NLT).

Application for today: The cloud of our sins and the mist of our transgressions have been removed forever by Christ's sacrificial death on Calvary's cross. Live today as if your debts to God have been paid!

Scripture for today (#106): Make sure nobody pays anyone back evil for evil. (1 Thessalonians 5:15a NTE).

Application for today: Instead, always find the way to do good to one another, and to everybody. (1 Thessalonians 5:15b NTE).

Scripture for today (#107): Yet true godliness with contentment is itself great wealth. After all, we brought nothing with us when we came into the world, and we can't take anything with us when we leave it. (1 Timothy 6:6-7 NLT).

Application for today: So if we have enough food and clothing, let us be content (1 Timothy 6:8 NLT).

Scripture for today (#108): Then Jesus stood up again and said to the woman, "Where are your accusers? Didn't even one of them condemn you?" "No, Lord," she said. And Jesus said, "Neither do I. Go and sin no more." (John 8:10-11 NLT).

Application for today: Who dares accuse us whom God has chosen for his own? No one—for God himself has given us right standing with himself. Who then will condemn us? No one—for Christ Jesus died for us and was raised to life for us, and he is sitting in the place of honor at God's right hand, pleading for us. (Romans 8:33-34 NLT).

God is on our side!

YOU + GOD = the MAJORITY (*the one math equation that solves all the other problems*)— Author Unknown

Scripture for today (#109): "For no one can come to me unless the Father who sent me draws them to me, and at the last day I will raise them up" —Jesus (John 6:44 NLT).

Application for today: For God knew His people in advance, and He chose them to become like His Son, so that His Son would be the firstborn among many brothers and sisters.

And having chosen them, He called them to come to Him. And having called them, He gave them right standing with Himself. And having given them right standing, He gave them His glory. (Romans 8:29-30 NLT).

Dear friends, we are already God's children, but He has not yet shown us what we will be like when Christ appears. But we do know that we will be like Him, for we will see Him as He really is. (1 John 3:2 NLT).

Scripture for today (#110): I have other sheep, too, that are not in this sheepfold. I must bring them also. They will listen to my voice, and there will be one flock with one shepherd. (John 10:16 NLT).

Application for today: Know this, although you were not a part of the original 12 disciples or the additional 72, Jesus had you in mind. He acknowledged in John 10:16 that you are a part of His Story. Listen to His voice. We are one flock with one Shepherd.

John 10:11 "I am the good shepherd. The good shepherd sacrifices his life for the sheep.— Jesus (NIV).

Scripture for today (#111): Jesus replied, "But even more blessed are all who hear the word of God and put it into practice." (Luke 11:28 NLT).

Application for today: But don't just listen to God's word. You must do what it says. Otherwise, you are only fooling yourselves. (James 1:22 NLT).

Scripture for today (#112): Then he added, "Son of man, let all my words sink deep into your own heart first. Listen to them carefully for yourself. Then go to your people in exile and say to them, 'This is what the Sovereign Lord says!' Do this whether they listen to you or not." (Ezekial 3:10-11 NLT).

Application for today: What a wonderful pattern set forth in scripture! *Before* we share the Word with others, let's make certain we have *first* shared it with ourselves. *Before* we attempt to teach, reprove, correct, or instruct others in righteousness, it behooves us to become a student *first*.

Scripture for today (#113): A good man brings good things out of the good stored up in his heart, and an evil man brings evil things out of the evil stored up in his heart. For the mouth speaks what the heart is full of. (Luke 6:45 NIV).

Application for today: Our words are like a thermometer that measure the warmth or chill in our hearts. Reset the thermostat of your heart today with the warmth of God's word and bring comfort to those around you with the words you speak. — Demario L. Rollins

Scripture for today (#114): "The Lord does not look at the things people look at. People look at the outward appearance, but the Lord looks at the heart." (1 Samuel 16:7b NIV).

Application for today: Don't allow the judgements people make about your outward appearance to dictate your attitude today. Permit the One who looks at your heart to be the source of your joy and the object of your worship. Build your hope on and around the Eternal One.

Scripture for today (#115): When Jesus saw that he had answered wisely, he said to him, "You are not far from the kingdom of God." And from then on no one dared ask him any more questions. (Mark 12:34 NIV).

Application for today: How the teacher of religious law answered Jesus is how we should strive to live life today and every day! Let's listen in to his conversation with Jesus below:

The teacher of religious law replied, "Well said, Teacher. You have spoken the truth by saying that there is only one God and no other. And I know it is important to love him with all my heart and all my understanding and all my strength, and to love my neighbor as myself. This is more important than to offer all of the burnt offerings and sacrifices required in the law." (Mark 12:32-33 NLT).

Let it be said of us by Jesus, "You are not far from the kingdom of God".

Scripture for today (#116): "At that time Michael, the great prince who protects your people, will arise. There will be a time of distress such as has not happened from the beginning of nations until then. But at that time your people—everyone whose name is found written in the book—will be delivered. (Daniel 12:1 NIV).

Application for today: Have you confessed your sins? Have you put your trust in the sacrifice of Jesus Christ? Have you put Jesus on in baptism? Has your name been written in the Lamb's Book of Life? Believer, I have wonderful news for you—everyone whose name is found written in the book—will be delivered!

> *And you also were included in Christ when you heard the message of truth, the gospel of your salvation. When you believed, you were marked in him with a seal, the promised Holy Spirit, who is a deposit guaranteeing our inheritance until the redemption of those who are God's possession—to the praise of his glory.* (Ephesians 1:13-14 NIV).

Scriptures for today (#117): Then the Lord said to Abraham, "Why did Sarah laugh and say, 'Will I really have a child, now that I am old?' **_Is anything too hard for the Lord_**? I will return to you at the appointed time next year, and Sarah will have a son." (Genesis 18:13-14 NIV).

The Lord said to Moses, **_"Is the Lord's hand (ability, power) limited (short, inadequate)_**? You shall see now whether My word will come to pass for you or not." (Numbers 11:23 The Amplified Bible).

Application for today: Then Jesus said, "Did I not tell you that **_if you believe, you will see_** the glory of God?" (John 11:40 NIV).

As Christians we don't have to see it to believe it. To repeat what The Teacher said, **_"If you believe, you will see"_**

(Note: **bold**, _italics_ and <u>underline</u> added for emphasis)

Scripture for today (#118): For there is nothing hidden that will not be disclosed, and nothing concealed that will not be known or brought out into the open. (Luke 8:17 NIV).

Application for today: Therefore judge nothing before the appointed time; wait until the Lord comes. He will bring to light what is hidden in darkness and will expose the motives of the heart. At that time each will receive their praise from God. (1 Corinthians 4:5 NIV).

Live a life of transparency today. Live a life of transparency tomorrow. Live a life of transparency every day. When the body you've been given ceases to exchange oxygen for carbon dioxide, let it be said of you that you lived a life of transparency.

Scripture for today (#119): They preached the gospel in that city and won a large number of disciples. Then they returned to Lystra, Iconium and Antioch, strengthening the disciples and encouraging them to remain true to the faith. "We must go through many hardships to enter the kingdom of God," they said. (Acts 14:21-22 NIV).

Application for today: Indeed, all who want to live a godly life in Christ Jesus will be persecuted. (2 Timothy 3:12 NRSV).

Matthew 5:10-12 NIV
"Blessed are those who are persecuted because of righteousness, for theirs is the kingdom of heaven. Blessed are you when people insult you, persecute you and falsely say all kinds of evil against you because of me. **Rejoice and be glad, because great is your reward in heaven,** for in the same way they persecuted the prophets who were before you".—Jesus

Scripture for today (#120): On the Sabbath we went outside the city gate to the river, where we expected to find a place of prayer. We sat down and began to speak to the women who had gathered there. One of those listening was a woman from the city of Thyatira named Lydia, a dealer in purple cloth. She was a worshiper of God. The Lord opened her heart to respond to Paul's message. (Acts 16:13-14 NIV).

Application for today: Sometimes God gives His children spectacular testimonies of conversion from a life of sin to a life of salvation. Other times, though still miraculous, the conversion process may be mysterious and amiable. Regardless of your conversion story, you are chosen and special to God. Live like a child of the Most High today!

Scripture for today (#121): As soon as it was night, the believers sent Paul and Silas away to Berea. On arriving there, they went to the Jewish synagogue. Now the Berean Jews were of more noble character than those in Thessalonica, for they received the message with great eagerness and examined the Scriptures every day to see if what Paul said was true. As a result, many of them believed, as did also a number of prominent Greek women and many Greek men. (Acts 17:10-12 NIV).

Application for today: Examine the Scriptures every day. Don't take a respected leader's explanation of the Scriptures as absolute truth. Take the time to dig into the Scriptures for yourself and discover what God wants to say to you today!

Scripture for today (#122): After these *events Paul* left Athens and went to Corinth. And he found a Jew named Aquila, a native of Pontus having recently come from Italy with his wife Priscilla, because Claudius had commanded all the Jews to leave Rome. He came to them, and because he was of the same trade he stayed with them, and they worked *together*, for they were tent-makers by trade. (Acts 18:1-3 NASB).

Application for today: Paul is regarded by many as one of the greatest Christians to have contributed to the Kingdom of God. Yet, he had a trade and made productive use of his hands. Feeling guilty because you're not in full time ministry? Don't! Enjoy your trade and make it your mission field.

Do your work, and be happy to do it. Work as if you were serving the Lord, not as if you were serving only men. (Ephesians 6:7 ICB).

Scripture for today (#123): "But one thing I do confess, that I believe in the way of salvation, which they refer to as a sect; I follow that system of serving the God of our ancestors; I firmly believe in the Jewish law and everything written in the books of prophecy; and I believe, just as these men do, that there will be a resurrection of both the righteous and ungodly. (Acts 24:14-15 The Living Bible).

Application for today: In view of this I also do my best to maintain a blameless conscience *both* before God and before *other* people, always. (Acts 24:16 NASB).

Jesus said, "Go and do the same." (Luke 10:37b The Message).

Scripture for today (#124): This is all the more urgent, for you know how late it is; time is running out. Wake up, for our salvation is nearer now than when we first believed. The night is almost gone; the day of salvation will soon be here. (Romans 13:11-12a NLT).

Application for today: So remove your dark deeds like dirty clothes, and put on the shining armor of right living. Because we belong to the day, we must live decent lives for all to see (Romans 13:12b-13a NLT).

Scripture for today (#125): But now God has shown us a way to be made right with him without keeping the requirements of the law, as was promised in the writings of Moses and the prophets long ago. (Romans 3:21 NLT).

Application for today: We are made right with God by placing our faith in Jesus Christ. And this is true for everyone who believes, no matter who we are. (Romans 3:22 NLT).

Scripture for today (#126): So if you eat, or if you drink, or if you do anything, do everything for the glory of God. Never do anything that might make others do wrong—Jews, Greeks, or God's church. I do the same thing. I try to please everybody in every way. I am not trying to do what is good for me. I try to do what is good for the most people. I do this so that they can be saved. (1 Corinthians 10:31-33 ICB).

Application for today: Do not *merely* look out for your own personal interests, but also for the interests of others. (Philippians 2:4 The Amplified Bible).

Do not look out only for yourselves. Look out for the good of others. (1 Corinthians 10:24 Expanded Bible).

Scripture for today (#127): We work together with God. So we are asking you not to receive God's grace and then do nothing with it. (2 Corinthians 6:1 NIRV).

Application for today: For God says, "At just the right time, I heard you. On the day of salvation, I helped you." Indeed, the "right time" is now. *Today* is the day of salvation. (2 Corinthians 6:2 NLT).

Today is the day to pray.
Today is the day to repent.
Today is the day to be saved.
Today is the day to love.
Today is the day to forgive.
Today is the day to live the life of salvation.

At just the right time, I will respond to you. On the day of salvation I will help you. (Isaiah 49:8 NLT).

Scripture for today (#128): For God made Christ, who never sinned, to be the offering for our sin, so that we could be made right with God through Christ. (2 Corinthians 5:21 NLT).

Application for today: Is this not the Great Exchange? God traded the filthiness of our sins for the faithfulness and perfection of Christ's righteousness!

Prayer:

Father, it is incomprehensible how Your love, grace, kindness, mercy, and favor pursue us even when we're not pursuing You.

We deserve Hell, You've promised us Heaven.
We deserve separation, You've promised
Your presence.
We deserve punishment, You've promised an inheritance.

Thank You for the unconditional grace extended to us through Your precious Son and our Wonderful Counselor. In Jesus' Name, Amen!

Scripture for today (#129): Clearly, Christ's love guides us. We are convinced of the fact that one man has died for all people. Therefore, all people have died. (2 Corinthians 5:14 God's Word Translation).

Application for today: He died for all, so that those who live should no longer live for themselves, but only for him who died and was raised to life for their sake. (2 Corinthians 5:15 GNT).

Live for Jesus today. Live for Him alone.

Scripture for today (#130): It is God himself, in his mercy, who has given us this wonderful work of telling his Good News to others, and so we never give up. (1 Corinthians 4:1 TLB).

Application for today: We don't do shameful things that must be kept secret. And we don't try to fool anyone or twist God's message around. God is our witness that we speak only the truth, so others will be sure that we can be trusted. (2 Corinthians 4:2 CEV).

Because of God's mercies and the assignment He has given us to share the Good News:

1. Don't do shameful things that must be kept secret.
2. Don't try to fool anyone.
3. Don't twist God's message around.
4. Acknowledge God's presence as your witness as you witness for Him.
5. Speak only the truth.
6. Be trustworthy.
7. Don't give up!

Scripture for today (#131): "But now your kingdom will not endure; the Lord has sought out a man after his own heart and appointed him ruler of his people, because you have not kept the Lord's command." (1 Samuel 13:14 NIV).

Application for today: When our hearts are going in the opposite direction of God's, like King Saul, eventually our little kingdom will fall apart. Choose to seek the heart of the Living God today and follow where He leads.

Scripture for today (#132): The heart is deceitful above all things and beyond cure. Who can understand it? "I the Lord search the heart and examine the mind, to reward each person according to their conduct, according to what their deeds deserve." (Jeremiah 17:9-10 NIV).

Application for today: Like a wild animal that is untamed, a heart without training and correction will naturally gravitate toward evil because of sin. Dive into God's Word today—it's the best remedy for the heart! Because...

God's Word is living and powerful. It is sharper than a sword that cuts both ways. It cuts straight into where the soul and spirit meet and it divides them. It cuts into the joints and bones. It tells what the heart is thinking about and what it wants to do. No one can hide from God. His eyes see everything we do. We must give an answer to God for what we have done.
(Hebrews 4:12-13 New Life Version).

Scriptures for today (#133): Above all else, guard your heart, for everything you do flows from it. (Proverbs 4:23 NIV).

A good person produces good out of the good stored up in his heart. An evil person produces evil out of the evil stored up in his heart, for his mouth speaks from the overflow of the heart. (Luke 6:45 Christian Standard Bible).

Application for today: Keep your mouth free of perversity; keep corrupt talk far from your lips. Let your eyes look straight ahead; fix your gaze directly before you. (Proverbs 4:24-25 NIV).

Scripture for today (#134): And this is the message I proclaim—that the day is coming when God, through Christ Jesus, will judge everyone's secret life. (Romans 2:16 NLT).

Application for today: For once you were full of darkness, but now you have light from the Lord. So live as people of light! For this light within you produces only what is good and right and true. Carefully determine what pleases the Lord. Take no part in the worthless deeds of evil and darkness; instead, expose them. It is shameful even to talk about the things that ungodly people do in secret. (Ephesians 5:8-12 NLT).

Scripture for today (#135): Confess your sins to each other and pray for each other so that you may be healed. The earnest prayer of a righteous person has great power and produces wonderful results. (James 5:16 NLT).

Application for today: Consider these actions today:

1. **Ask** someone how you can pray for them.
2. **Tell** someone else how they can pray for you.
3. **Confess** your sins to someone you trust.
4. **Offer** to be a confidant to someone who trusts you.
5. **Create** a prayer journal and keep track of God's answers.

Scripture for today (#136): In his grace, God has given us different gifts for doing certain things well. So if God has given you the ability to prophesy, speak out with as much faith as God has given you. (Romans 12:6 NLT).

Application for today: If your gift is serving others, serve them well. If you are a teacher, teach well. If your gift is to encourage others, be encouraging. If it is giving, give generously. If God has given you leadership ability, take the responsibility seriously. And if you have a gift for showing kindness to others, do it gladly. (Romans 12:7-8 NLT).

Scripture for today (#137): A spiritual gift is given to each of us so we can help each other. (1 Corinthians 12:7 NLT).

Application for today: To one person the Spirit gives the ability to give wise advice; to another the same Spirit gives a message of special knowledge. The same Spirit gives great faith to another, and to someone else the one Spirit gives the gift of healing. He gives one person the power to perform miracles, and another the ability to prophesy. He gives someone else the ability to discern whether a message is from the Spirit of God or from another spirit. Still another person is given the ability to speak in unknown languages, while another is given the ability to interpret what is being said. It is the one and only Spirit who distributes all these gifts. He alone decides which gift each person should have. (1 Corinthians 12:8-11 NLT).

Use your gift(s) today to help each other.

Scripture for today (#138): God has given each of you a gift from his great variety of spiritual gifts. Use them well to serve one another. (1 Peter 4:10 NLT).

Application for today: Do you have the gift of speaking? Then speak as though God himself were speaking through you. Do you have the gift of helping others? Do it with all the strength and energy that God supplies. Then everything you do will bring glory to God through Jesus Christ. All glory and power to him forever and ever! Amen. (1 Peter 4:11 NLT).

Scripture for today (#139): Be thankful in all circumstances, for this is God's will for you who belong to Christ Jesus. (1 Thessalonians 5:18 NLT).

Application for today: Over the next several minutes, think about some things you're grateful for (10 to 20 items will be sufficient). Make a list and check it twice. Pray and thank God for what you've written. Meditate on your list often throughout the day. Make this a habit. This is God's will for you who belong to Christ Jesus.

Scripture for today (#140): Make the most of every opportunity in these evil days. (Ephesians 5:16 NLT).

Application for today: Today, focus on **"The List"**. This is a list of 5 activities you feel like you "should" be doing in your "personal" quest to be a disciple of Jesus Christ. The activities you list are personal nudges you get on the inside from the Holy Spirit as He encourages you to follow Jesus.

Demario's List:
1. Witness to the Lost.
2. Disciple a Believer.
3. Teach God's Word.
4. Give Generously.
5. Prayer with the Almighty.

After you make your list, dare yourself to "DO" something on your list before the sun goes down. Meditate on your list often throughout the day. Make this a habit.

Jesus said to his followers, "There is such a big harvest of people to bring in. But there are only a few workers to help harvest them. God owns the harvest.

Ask him to send more workers to help gather his harvest." (Matthew 9:37-38 ERV).

My prayer is that our lists will drive us out of our comfort zones and into the harvest to help with the great work God is doing!

Scripture for today (#141): When God's people are in need, be ready to help them. Always be eager to practice hospitality. (Romans 12:13 NLT).

Application for today: Today we're going to take the **S.M.O.A.S.** challenge. Your mission over the next 12 hours is to find an opportunity to **S**pend **M**oney **O**n **A S**tranger—(5 to 10 dollars will be sufficient). The best scenario is to personally present this money to someone you have never met, perhaps at a grocery store or gas station. When the person asks why you would do such a thing, you respond: *"All that I have belongs to Jesus Christ and He placed it on my heart to share this with you. How can I pray for you or your family today?"* If more needs to be said, the Holy Spirit will guide your thoughts and words.

And don't forget to do good and to share with those in need. These are the sacrifices that please God. (Hebrews 13:16 NLT).

Scripture for today (#142): _Put away the old person_ you used to be. Have nothing to do with your old sinful life. It was sinful because of being fooled into following bad desires. (Ephesians 4:22 NLV).

Application for today: Instead, let the Spirit renew your thoughts and attitudes. _Put on your new nature_, created to be like God—truly righteous and holy. (Ephesians 4:23-24 NLT).

(Note: _Italics_ added for emphasis)

Scripture for today (#143): "There will always be temptations to sin," Jesus said one day to his disciples (Luke 17:1a TLB).

Application for today: No temptation has come your way that is too hard for flesh and blood to bear. But God can be trusted not to allow you to suffer any temptation beyond your powers of endurance. He will see to it that every temptation has a way out, so that it will never be impossible for you to bear it. (1 Corinthians 10:13 J.B. Phillips New Testament).

Dear Friends, the bad news is that temptations are sure to come today. The good news is that God has a plan.

As the movie theater is sure to have an EXIT sign prominently displayed in the darkness of its atmosphere, so has the Master of the Universe fixed an escape hatch from our temptation. God's Word promises an EXIT door...it's up to us to find it and use it!—Demario L. Rollins

Scripture for today (#144): When I am with those who are weak, I **_share_** their weakness, for I want to bring the weak to Christ. Yes, I try to find common ground with everyone, doing everything I can to save some.I do everything to spread the Good News and share in its blessings. (1 Corinthians 9:22-23 NLT).

Application for today: **_Carry_** one another's burdens; in this way you will fulfill the law of Christ. (Galatians 6:2 CSB)

Share in someone's weakness today. **_Carry_** someone's burden today.

Through the acts of **"_sharing_"** and **"_carrying_"**, God can open doors to unbelieving hearts—Demario L. Rollins

(Note: **bold**, _italics_ and underline added for emphasis)

Scripture for today (#145): The sinful self wants what is against the Spirit, and the Spirit wants what is against the sinful self. They are always fighting against each other, so that you don't do what you really want to do. (Galatians 5:17 ERV).

Application for today: So I tell you: Live by following the Spirit. Then you will not do what your sinful selves want. (Galatians 5:16 NCV).

Hypothetical Example:

Dog A: Hubert

Dog B: Harry

Inquisition: If you feed Hubert and neglect Harry, which dog would win if they got into a heated disagreement which led to physical conflict?

Answer: Hubert would win because he has been well nourished.

Extrapolation: Feed Hubert (Spirit) and neglect Harry (flesh). When they get into a heated disagreement, Hubert (Spirit) will win because of the spiritual nourishment from God's Word.

Bonus scripture: Good people take care of their animals, but wicked people are cruel to theirs. (Proverbs 12:10 GNT).

Scripture for today (#146): For you know quite well that the day of the Lord's return will come unexpectedly, like a thief in the night. When people are saying, "Everything is peaceful and secure," then disaster will fall on them as suddenly as a pregnant woman's labor pains begin. And there will be no escape. (1 Thessalonians 5:2-3 NLT).

Application for today: But you aren't in the dark about these things, dear brothers and sisters, and you won't be surprised when the day of the Lord comes like a thief. For you are all children of the light and of the day; we don't belong to darkness and night. So be on your guard, not asleep like the others. Stay alert and be clearheaded. (1 Thessalonians 5:4-6 NLT).

Scripture for today (#147): Teach those who are rich in this world not to be proud and not to trust in their money, which is so unreliable. (1 Timothy 6:17a NLT).

Application for today: Their trust should be in God, who richly gives us all we need for our enjoyment. (1 Timothy 6:17b NLT).

Tell them to use their money to do good. They should be rich in good works and generous to those in need, always being ready to share with others. By doing this they will be storing up their treasure as a good foundation for the future so that they may experience true life. (1 Timothy 6:18-19 NLT).

For we must all appear before the judgment seat of the Messiah, so that each may receive what has been done through the body, whether good or bad. (2 Corinthians 5:10 NTE).

Scripture for today (#148): Keep a close watch on how you live and on your teaching. (1 Timothy 4:16a NLT).

Application for today: Stay true to what is right for the sake of your own salvation and the salvation of those who hear you. (1 Timothy 4:16b NLT).

For we [believers will be called to account and] must all appear before the judgment seat of Christ, so that each one may be repaid for what has been done in the body, whether good or bad [that is, each will be held responsible for his actions, purposes, goals, motives—the use or misuse of his time, opportunities and abilities]. (2 Corinthians 5:10 Amplified Bible).

Scripture for today (#149): Don't let anyone think less of you because you are young. (1 Timothy 4:12a NLT).

Application for today: Be an example to all believers in what you say, in the way you live, in your love, your faith, and your purity. (1 Timothy 4:12b NLT).

We must all stand before Christ to be judged. Everyone will get what they should. They will be paid for whatever they did—good or bad—when they lived in this earthly body. (2 Corinthians 5:10 ERV).

Scripture for today (#150): Do not waste time arguing over godless ideas and old wives' tales. (1 Timothy 4:7a NLT).

Application for today: Instead, train yourself to be godly. "Physical training is good, but training for godliness is much better, promising benefits in this life and in the life to come." (1 Timothy 4:7b-8 NLT).

Sooner or later we'll all have to face God, regardless of our conditions. We will appear before Christ and take what's coming to us as a result of our actions, either good or bad.

(2 Corinthians 5:10 The Message).

Scripture for today (#151): 'Didn't I tell you', said Jesus, 'that if you believed you would see God's glory?' (John 11:40 New Testament for Everyone Version).

Application for today: It fascinates me how big the Earth is. The sun is even larger. And the Universe…we have no measurement whatsoever for its size. God. Infinite. By deduction, we know He is bigger than our problems, but when we hold them so close to our face it tends to block our view of Him. As our thumb can eclipse the airplane in the sky, our problems can eclipse the splendor and power of our Great God if we let them. — Demario L. Rollins

Scriptures for today (#152): Make allowance for each other's faults, and forgive anyone who offends you. (Colossians 3:13a NLT).

Always be humble and gentle. Be patient with each other, making allowance for each other's faults because of your love. (Ephesians 4:2 NLT).

Application for today: Remember, the Lord forgave you, so you must forgive others. (Colossians 3:13b NLT).

Above all, clothe yourselves with love, which binds us all together in perfect harmony. And let the peace that comes from Christ rule in your hearts. For as members of one body you are called to live in peace. And always be thankful. (Colossians 3:14-15 NLT).

Scripture for today (#153): He erased the certificate of debt, with its obligations, that was against us and opposed to us, and has taken it away by nailing it to the cross. (Colossians 2:14 CSB).

Application for today: He defeated the rulers and powers of the spiritual world. With the cross he won the victory over them and led them away, as defeated and powerless prisoners for the whole world to see. (Colossians 2:15 ERV).

Then I heard a great voice in Heaven cry: "Now the salvation and the power and kingdom of our God, and the authority of his Christ have come! For the accuser of our brethren has been thrown down from this place, where he stood before our God accusing them day and night. Now they have conquered him through the blood of the Lamb, and through the Word to which they bore witness. They did not cherish life even in the face of death! (Revelation 12:10-11 J.B. Phillips New Testament).

We're on the winning team. Live like it. Today. And everyday!

Scripture for today (#154): Dirty stories, foul talk, and coarse jokes—these are not for you. (Ephesians 5:4a TLB).

Application for today: Instead, remind each other of God's goodness, and be thankful. (Ephesians 5:4b TLB).

You can be sure of this: The Kingdom of Christ and of God will never belong to anyone who is impure or greedy, for a greedy person is really an idol worshiper—he loves and worships the good things of this life more than God. Don't be fooled by those who try to excuse these sins, for the terrible wrath of God is upon all those who do them. (Ephesians 5:5-6 TLB).

Scripture for today (#155): So the promise is received by faith. It is given as a free gift. And we are all certain to receive it, whether or not we live according to the law of Moses, if we have faith like Abraham's. For Abraham is the father of all who believe. That is what the Scriptures mean when God told him, "I have made you the father of many nations." This happened because Abraham believed in the God who brings the dead back to life and who creates new things out of nothing. (Romans 4:16-17 NLT).

Application for today: Hebrews 11:1 (multiple translations)

Now faith is assurance of things hoped for, proof of things not seen. (WEB)

Now faith is *the* certainty of *things* hoped for, a proof of things not seen. (NASB)

Now faith is the reality of what is hoped for, the proof of what is not seen. (HCSB)

Now faith is the substance of things hoped for, the evidence of things not seen. (KJV)

Now faith is the assurance of things hoped for, the conviction of things not seen. (RSV)

Now faith is being sure of what we hope for, being convinced of what we do not see. (NET)

Faith shows the reality of what we hope for; it is the evidence of things we cannot see. (NLT)

Now faith is the assurance (title deed, confirmation) of things hoped for (divinely guaranteed), and the evidence of things not seen [the conviction of their reality—faith comprehends as fact what cannot be experienced by the physical senses]. (Amplified Bible).

Scripture for today (#156): For everything comes from him and exists by his power and is intended for his glory. All glory to him forever! Amen. (Romans 11:36 NLT)

Application for today:

Your name goes here	comes from God.
Your name goes here	exists by God's power.
Your name goes here	is intended for God's glory.
Your name goes here	must give all glory to God forever!

Isaiah 42:8 GNT "I alone am the Lord your God. No other god may share my glory; I will not let idols share my praise.

Scripture for today (#157): When one of you has a dispute with another believer, how dare you file a lawsuit and ask a secular court to decide the matter instead of taking it to other believers! Don't you realize that someday we believers will judge the world? And since you are going to judge the world, can't you decide even these little things among yourselves? Don't you realize that we will judge angels? So you should surely be able to resolve ordinary disputes in this life. (1 Corinthians 6:1-3 NLT).

Application for today:

Part 1: Avoid lawsuits with Christians

Part 2: We know very little about our full service responsibilities to the Master of the Universe in the life to come. However, this passage of scripture gives us a glimpse into a couple of roles our inheritance has granted to us by the Grace of Jesus Christ. How mysteriously wonderful that we should be partakers in judging matters of the world to come!

God's riches, wisdom, and knowledge are so deep! They are as mysterious as his judgments, and they are as hard to track as his paths! (Romans 11:33 CEB).

Scripture for today (#158): Don't you realize that your body is the temple of the Holy Spirit, who lives in you and was given to you by God? You do not belong to yourself, for God bought you with a high price. So you must honor God with your body. (1 Corinthians 6:19-20 NLT).

Application for today: Run away from immorality. Every sin that it's possible for someone to commit happens outside the body; but immorality involves sinning against your own body. (1 Corinthians 6:18 New Testament for Everyone).

God paid a high price for you, so don't be enslaved by the world. (1 Corinthians 7:23 NLT).

Scripture for today (#159): I assure you that they gave what they could afford and even more than they could afford, and they did it voluntarily. (2 Corinthians 8:3 CEB).

Who: Churches in Macedonia (verse 1)
Circumstances: tested by many troubles (verse 2)
Economic status: very poor (verse 2)
Disposition: filled with abundant joy (verse 2)
Verbal communication: begged again and again to share (verse 4)

How could a poor group of people who are tested by many troubles beg again and again for the privilege of sharing in a gift for others?

They even did more than we had hoped, for **their first action** was to give themselves to the Lord and to us, just as God wanted them to do. (2 Corinthians 8:5 NLT).

Application for today: Being filled with abundant joy overflows in rich generosity. Giving ourselves wholeheartedly to God and his ambassadors makes it possible for cheerful giving to occur.

You must each decide in your heart how much to give. And don't give reluctantly or in response to pressure. "For God loves a person who gives cheerfully." (2 Corinthians 9:7 NLT).
(Note: **Bold** print added for emphasis)

Scripture for today (#160): But I am not surprised! Even Satan disguises himself as an angel of light. So it is no wonder that his servants also disguise themselves as servants of righteousness. In the end they will get the punishment their wicked deeds deserve. (2 Corinthians 11:14-15 NLT).

Application for today: Dear friends, do not believe everyone who claims to speak by the Spirit. You must test them to see if the spirit they have comes from God. For there are many false prophets in the world. This is how we know if they have the Spirit of God: If a person claiming to be a prophet acknowledges that Jesus Christ came in a real body, that person has the Spirit of God. But if someone claims to be a prophet and does not acknowledge the truth about Jesus, that person is not from God. Such a person has the spirit of the Antichrist, which you heard is coming into the world and indeed is already here. But you belong to God, my dear children. You have already won a victory over those people, because the Spirit who lives in you is greater than the spirit who lives in the world. Those people belong to this world, so they speak from the world's viewpoint, and the world listens to them. But we belong to God, and those who know God listen to us. If they do not belong to God, they do not listen to us.

That is how we know if someone has the Spirit of truth or the spirit of deception. (1 John 4:1-6 NLT).

Scripture for today (#161): In a wealthy home some utensils are made of gold and silver, and some are made of wood and clay. The expensive utensils are used for special occasions, and the cheap ones are for everyday use. (2 Timothy 2:20 NLT).

Application for today: The Lord wants to use you for special purposes, so make yourself clean from all evil. Then you will be holy, and the Master can use you. You will be ready for any good work. (2 Timothy 2:21 ERV).

Scripture for today (#162): By his divine power, God has given us everything we need for living a godly life. We have received all of this by coming to know him, the one who called us to himself by means of his marvelous glory and excellence. And because of his glory and excellence, he has given us great and precious promises. These are the promises that enable you to share his divine nature and escape the world's corruption caused by human desires. (2 Peter 1:3-4 NLT).

Application for today: In view of all this, make every effort to respond to God's promises. Supplement your faith with a generous provision of moral excellence, and moral excellence with knowledge, and knowledge with self-control, and self-control with patient endurance, and patient endurance with godliness, and godliness with brotherly affection, and brotherly affection with love for everyone. The more you grow like this, the more productive and useful you will be in your knowledge of our Lord Jesus Christ. (2 Peter 1:5-8 NLT).

Scripture for today (#163): The end of the world is near. (1 Peter 4:7a NLV).

Application for today: Therefore, be earnest and disciplined in your prayers. Most important of all, continue to show deep love for each other, for love covers a multitude of sins. Cheerfully share your home with those who need a meal or a place to stay. (1 Peter 4:7b-9 NLT).

Scripture for today (#164): For you know that God paid a ransom to save you from the empty life you inherited from your ancestors. And it was not paid with mere gold or silver, which lose their value. It was the precious blood of Christ, the sinless, spotless Lamb of God. (1 Peter 1:18 NLT).

Application for today: [9]*ransom* [**ran**-suhm] 1. the redemption of a prisoner or kidnapped person, of captured goods, etc., for a price.

---

[9] Dictionary.com Online, s.v. "ransom," accessed December 10, 2020, https://www.dictionary.com/browse/ransom?s=t

[10]*Redemption* [ri-**demp**-shu*hn*] 1. an act of redeeming or atoning for a fault or mistake

[11]*Redeem* [ri-**deem**] 1. to buy or pay off; clear by payment

[12]*Atone* [*uh*-**tohn**] 1. to make amends or reparation, as for an offense or a crime, or for an offender

Feeling unworthy today? God paid a high price for you! You are more valuable than you realize!

Let us praise God for his glorious grace, for the free gift he gave us in his dear Son! (Ephesians 1:6 GNT).

Scripture for today (#165): "Again, you have heard that it was said to the people long ago, 'Do not break your oath, but fulfill to the Lord the vows you have made.' But I tell you, do not swear an oath at all:either by heaven, for it is God's throne; or by the earth,

---

[10] Dictionary.com Online, s.v. "redemption," accessed December 10, 2020, https://www.dictionary.com/browse/redemption?s=t

[11] Dictionary.com Online, s.v. "redeem," accessed December 10, 2020, https://www.dictionary.com/browse/redeem?s=t

[12] Dictionary.com Online, s.v. "atone," accessed December 10, 2020, https://www.dictionary.com/browse/atone?s=t

for it is his footstool; or by Jerusalem, for it is the city of the Great King. And do not swear by your head, for you cannot make even one hair white or black. All you need to say is simply 'Yes' or 'No'; anything beyond this comes from the evil one. (Matthew 5:33-37 NIV).

Application for today: It is of the highest importance, my brothers, that your speech should be free from oaths (whether they are "by" heaven or earth or anything else). Your yes should be a plain yes, and your no a plain no, and then you cannot go wrong in the matter. (James 5:12 J.B. Phillips New Testament Version).

Scripture for today (#166): Just a moment, now, you who say, "We are going to such-and-such a city today or tomorrow. We shall stay there a year doing business and make a profit"! How do you know what will happen even tomorrow? What, after all, is your life? It is like a puff of smoke visible for a little while and then dissolving into thin air. (James 4:13-14 J.B. Phillips New Testament Version).

Application for today: Instead, make it a habit to say, "If the Master wills it and we're still alive, we'll do this or that." (James 4:15 The Message).

People might make many plans, but what the Lord says is what will happen. (Proverbs 19:21 ERV).

A man's heart plans his way, but the Lord determines his steps. (Proverbs 16:9 HCSB).

Scripture for today (#167): "If you [really] love Me, you will keep *and* obey My commandments. (John 14:15 Amplified Bible).

Application for today: If you are wise and understand God's ways, prove it by living an honorable life, doing good works with the humility that comes from wisdom. (James 3:13 NLT).

Scripture for today (#168): You, my brothers and sisters, were called to be free.(Galatians 5:13a NIV).

Application for today: Just make sure that you don't use this freedom as an excuse to do whatever you want to do and destroy your freedom. Rather, use your freedom to serve one another in love; that's how freedom grows. For everything we know about God's Word is summed up in a single sentence: Love others as you love yourself. (Galatians 5:13b-14 The Message).

Scripture for today (#169): Everyone has sinned and fallen short of God's glorious standard (Romans 3:23 NCV).

Application for today: If we say that we have no sin, we deceive ourselves, and the truth is not in us. If we confess our sins, he is faithful and just to forgive us our sins, and to cleanse us from all unrighteousness. If we say that we have not sinned, we make him a liar, and his word is not in us. (1 John 1:8-10 King James Version).

Scripture for today (#170): If someone claims, "I know God," but doesn't obey God's commandments, that person is a liar and is not living in the truth. (1 John 2:4 NLT).

Application for today: But if someone obeys God's teaching, then God's love has truly arrived at its goal in him. This is how we know that we are following God: Whoever says that God lives in him must live as Jesus lived. (1 John 2:5-6 ICB).

Scripture for today (#171): These people left our churches, but they never really belonged with us; otherwise they would have stayed with us. When they left, it proved that they did not belong with us. (1 John 2:19 NLT).

Application for today: People fall into one of two categories. Saved or Lost. There is no in-between. Those who have "fallen away" were perhaps never truly "born again":

You, however, are not in the realm of the flesh but are in the realm of the Spirit, if indeed the Spirit of God lives in you. And if anyone does not have the Spirit of Christ, they do not belong to Christ. (Romans 8:9 NIV).

Pay close attention to yourself [concentrate on your personal development] and to your teaching; persevere in these things [hold to them], for as you do this you will ensure salvation both for yourself and for those who hear you. (1 Timothy 4:16 The Amplified Bible).

Now it is God who makes both us and you stand firm in Christ. He anointed us, set his seal of ownership on us, and put his Spirit in our hearts as a deposit, guaranteeing what is to come. (2 Corinthians 1:22-23 NIV).

Scripture for today (#172): Therefore if anyone is in Christ [that is, grafted in, joined to Him by faith in Him as Savior], *he is* a new creature [reborn and renewed by the Holy Spirit]; the old things [the previous moral and spiritual condition] have passed away. Behold, new things have come [because spiritual awakening brings a new life]. (2 Corinthians 5:17 The Amplified Bible).

Application for today: They have been given God's Spirit (1 John 4:13) and have been sealed (Ephesians 1:13). The miracle and beauty of being truly born again is that the relationship remains even when the fellowship is broken. An example of this would be the prodigal son (Luke 15:11-32). Though he severed the *"fellowship"* he enjoyed with his father, he did not and could not sever the *"relationship"*. Though his actions were contrary to the will of his father, they were incapable of terminating the truth of the father-son relationship. When the son repented, he was welcomed with open arms.

Scripture for today (#173): The Lord isn't really being slow about his promise, as some people think. No, he is being patient for your sake. He does not want anyone to be destroyed, but wants everyone to repent. (2 Peter 3:9 NLT).

Application for today: God is withholding the return of Jesus to give His "creation" time to accept the invitation to become His "children".

C ongratulations on 173 days of solid commitment and devotion to practicing the presence of God through daily meditation on His Word. I now want to leave you with 10 final devotionals prepared in a slightly different format than what you've experienced thus far. Instead of a scripture and application, I will present a title followed by thoughts I encourage you to ponder. Go as deep as the Holy Spirit will take you! —Demario L. Rollins

The Pit Stop (#174): During a NASCAR race, drivers do hundreds of laps at incredible speeds, but the seconds spent during a pit stop may be the most essential moments of any race. In the pits, the vehicle stops for refueling, repairs, mechanical adjustments, or any combination of the aforementioned. Regardless of the driver's skill or the integrity of the vehicle, the pit stop is crucial. Perhaps you feel like you're stuck in a pit right now. During the race of life, we do thousands of days living under incredible stress, but the hours spent during the "pit stops" of life may be the most essential moments of this race called "life". In the pits, we stop to refuel, repair, adjust, or any combination of the aforementioned. Regardless of our skills or the integrity of our human frame, the pit stops of life are crucial. Don't be afraid of the road bumps and detours of life, our God prunes (John 15:2) and our God chastens (Hebrews 12:6).

When Your Walls Are Down (#175): In the Old Testament, walls surrounded Jerusalem. The walls provided the Israelites with protection, dignity, and a constant reminder that God was with His people. When the wall was not present, the people experienced shame and were left defenseless against their enemies. Wild animals, foreigners, or other opposition could easily enter the city and cause great trouble for them. Essentially, they were completely vulnerable to an innumerable amount of anomalies. It is not a stretch of the imagination to assume that the people felt exposed and abandoned by the God of their ancestors. Perhaps that is why Isaiah writes, "But Zion said, *"The Lord has forsaken me, the Lord has forgotten me." Can a mother forget the baby at her breast and have no compassion on the child she has borne? Though she may forget, I will not forget you! See, I have engraved you on the palms of my hands; your walls are ever before me.* (Isaiah 49:14-16 NIV). Dear reader, you may feel completely vulnerable to an innumerable amount of anomalies. It may even feel like you have been forsaken and even forgotten by the God you know. He has said that He will never forget you. He has you engraved on the palm of His hand. What a precious thought! Your walls, the very extent of your life, are ever before Him. Before you pray, He knows what you're going to say. Before you ask, He has an answer.

Why art thou cast down, O my soul? and why art thou disquieted in me? hope thou in God: for I shall yet praise him for the help of His countenance. (Psalm 42:5 KJV).

Why art thou cast down, O my soul? and why art thou disquieted within me? hope thou in God: for I shall yet praise him, who is the health of my countenance, and my God. (Psalm 42:11 KJV).

Why art thou cast down, O my soul? and why art thou disquieted within me? hope in God: for I shall yet praise him, who is the health of my countenance, and my God. (Psalm 43:5 KJV).

Breathe (#176): Imagine a gentleman named Sylar has a flame of fire burning on a torch. He is the only human on the planet that has ever seen or experienced this phenomenon called fire. Remi comes by with an unlit torch and Sylar is kind enough to share his flame. Now there are two people with fire! Remi shares his flame with Kael and Kael shares his flame with Heston who shares with Tallon who shares with Vino, who shares with Daxx. One day Daxx meets Rei who asks, where did your flame come from? Daxx says, "Vino". But actually, Daxx's flame came from Sylar!

Imagine a loving God who created Adam from the dust of the ground and breathed into his nostrils the breath of life, and Adam became a living being. He is the only human on the planet who has ever seen or experienced this phenomenon called life. God makes Eve from Adam, Eve gives birth to Cain, Abel, and Seth and the story goes on to include you, the reader. And then the author of this book asks, where did you get your breath of life from? Would the reader say his or her mother or father's name? Actually, the reader's breath of life came from God!

It's His breath in our lungs!

From one man He made all the nations, that they should inhabit the whole earth; and He marked out their appointed times in history and the boundaries of their lands. God did this so that they would seek Him and perhaps reach out for Him and find Him, though He is not far from any one of us. For in Him we live and move and have our being. As some of your own poets have said, "We are His offspring" (Acts 17:26-28 NIV).

Restoring the Garden (#177):

Adam was created and placed in a Garden. (Genesis 2:7-8).

Adam betrayed God in a Garden. (Genesis 3:6).

Adam was banished from a Garden. (Genesis 3:23).

The second Adam (1 Corinthians 15:45) met frequently with his disciples in a Garden. (John 18:2).

The second Adam (Jesus) prayed fervently concerning the plan of salvation in a Garden. (Luke 22:44).

Jesus was betrayed in a Garden. (Luke 22:48).

Jesus was crucified near a Garden. (John 19:41).

Jesus was buried and rose again near a Garden. (John 19:41; 20:15).

Jesus "restored" hope to a lost human race in the same sweet place we caused our downfall.

Thank you Father for restoring the Garden!

Best Christmas Ever (#178): Think about your best Christmas ever. The one gift you really wanted was wrapped very carefully in a beautiful package perhaps with a bow, ribbon, and a tag with your name on it. Although the wrapping paper was carefully picked out, the magic tape placed carefully, and the bow affixed to perfection, your ONLY interest was the gift inside. Nothing else mattered from the outside. And, if your gift wasn't inside, none of the outer wrappings would come close to the pleasure and excitement you expect to get from seeing and experiencing the toy or gift inside that you always wanted. If your gift had ears I could imagine you saying "*I don't' want it if you're not in it, I just want you*". There are MANY distractions in this world that constantly tempt us to be satisfied with the temporal fulfillment they give. Take the time today and every day to look for Jesus in every moment. If He's not in it, give it up and move on.

Psalm 42:1-2 (NLT) As the deer pants for streams of water, so my soul pants for you, my God.² My soul thirsts for God, for the living God. When can I go and meet with God?

Psalm 63:1 (NLT) You, God, are my God, earnestly I seek you; I thirst for you, my whole being longs for you, in a dry and parched land where there is no water.

Hebrews 11:6 (NLT) And without faith it is impossible to please God, because anyone who comes to him must believe that he exists and that he rewards those who earnestly seek him.

Everybody likes Surprises....right? (#179):

I remember being in school and the teacher would give us a syllabus at the beginning of the semester. In the syllabus, the teacher would outline everything that was expected in the weeks to come. It would describe chapters, topics, quizzes, tests, exams, final exams, and even breaks we'd have. Those who actually looked at the syllabus and followed it were prepared for what was to come. For those who ignored, lost, or misplaced their syllabus, the tests seemed _unfair_ and _unexpected_ because these students were totally unprepared to take them. For those who followed the syllabus, there were no surprises! The Bible is "like" a syllabus in that it outlines what we can expect out of this life so that we aren't surprised.

1 Peter 4:12-13 (NIV) Dear friends, do not be surprised at the fiery ordeal that has come on you to test you, as though something strange were happening to you. But rejoice inasmuch as you participate in the sufferings of Christ, so that you may be overjoyed when his glory is revealed.

That's Not Fair! (#180): I can remember playing basketball with my daughter when she was 5 years old. I was taller, faster, older, smarter, and better at basketball than she was. I could have probably stood at the goal and hit bank shots from under the net all day long. However, does that mean I should have unleashed my full potential on my daughter to show her who's boss? No, it doesn't. So, what did I do? Although I knew I could beat her, I dribbled and lost the ball. I missed shots on purpose. I fell down. I let her steal the ball. I would even get so tired (supposedly) that I could barely move. In games where 10 points would win, I would maybe get 7 points but she'd end up winning. Why did I do that? Because I love her. Because I wanted her to win. Because I wanted her to have confidence in herself. Because I didn't want her to give up and quit. There's no way she could have won unless she was given some kind of help. The writer of Hebrews in chapter twelve portrays life as a race and there's no way we can win at life unless we're given some kind of help. Perhaps you can think of several ways your life isn't fair. I can think of several ways Jesus makes up for it!

1 Peter 3:18 (NIV)
For Christ also suffered once for sins, the righteous for the unrighteous, to bring you to God. He was put to death in the body but made alive in the Spirit.

2 Corinthians 5:18-19 (NIV) All this is from God, who reconciled us to himself through Christ and gave us the ministry of reconciliation: that God was reconciling the world to himself in Christ, not counting people's sins against them. And he has committed to us the message of reconciliation.

Romans 5:8 (NIV)
But God demonstrates his own love for us in this: While we were still sinners, Christ died for us.

Psalm 103:11-12 (NIV)
For as high as the heavens are above the earth, so great is his love for those who fear him; as far as the east is from the west, so far has he removed our transgressions from us.

Hebrews 10:16-17 (NIV) "This is the covenant I will make with them after that time, says the Lord. I will put my laws in their hearts, and I will write them on their minds." Then he adds: "Their sins and lawless acts I will remember no more."

Romans 4:23-24 (NIV) The words "it was credited to him" were written not for him alone, but also for us, to whom God will credit righteousness—for us who believe in him who raised Jesus our Lord from the dead.

Isaiah 53:4-5 (NIV) Surely he took up our pain and bore our suffering, yet we considered him punished by God, stricken by him, and afflicted. But he was pierced for our transgressions, he was crushed for our iniquities; the punishment that brought us peace was on him, and by his wounds we are healed.

We Walk By Faith (#181): Which came first...God or the Earth? Which came first...the invisible or the visible? Which will outlast the other...God or the Earth? Which will last longer...the invisible or the visible? Could it be that what we think is true, certain, tangible, and real is actually but a passing expression of God's wonderful creation? Could it be that the "invisible" is what we should consider true, faithful, trustworthy, and "real"? Invisible things were here before visible things were created and they will be here after physical things have been consumed by God's wrath. Perhaps what we can't see, and what we believe by faith should be what we believe is "true". We walk by Faith and not by sight (2 Corinthians 5:7).

You are the Battlefield (#182): There are two who desperately want you. Jesus wants greatly to *save* you. Satan wants frantically to *sabotage* you. There's fierce love and ferocious hatred. All for you. You are the battlefield. They both want you. To whom will you pledge allegiance? This decision must be made hourly. To make no decision at all is actually a decision to choose Satan. No resistance is to give control to the enemy. Be sober, be vigilant; because your adversary the devil, as a roaring lion, walketh about, seeking whom he may devour (1 Peter 5:8 KJV). Just a partially opened door or one misstep will do. Give him but an inch and he will proceed to be your ruler. Stand. Fight. Watch and pray so that you will not fall into temptation. The spirit is willing, but the flesh is weak." (Matthew 26:41 NIV). Resist and he will flee (James 4:7). Greater is He that is in you than he that is in the world (1 John 4:4). You are a mighty warrior Gideon (Judges 6:12). You are who He says you are!

Three Important Questions (#183):

What really matters? Salvation, having your name in the Book of Life

Revelation 20:11-15 The Message (MSG)
I saw a Great White Throne and the One Enthroned. Nothing could stand before or against the Presence, nothing in Heaven, nothing on earth. And then I saw all the dead, great and small, standing there—before the Throne! And books were opened. Then another book was opened: the Book of Life. The dead were judged by what was written in the books, by the way they had lived. Sea released its dead, Death and Hell turned in their dead. Each man and woman was judged by the way he or she had lived. Then Death and Hell were hurled into Lake Fire. This is the second death—Lake Fire. Anyone whose name was not found inscribed in the Book of Life was hurled into Lake Fire.

How do I know I'm saved? The Holy Spirit, your engagement ring.

Ephesians 1:13-14 The Passion Translation (TPT)

And because of him, when you *who are not Jews* heard the revelation of truth, you believed in the wonderful news of salvation. Now we have been stamped with the seal of the promised Holy Spirit. He is given to us like an engagement ring is given to a bride, as the first installment of what's coming! He is our hope-promise of a future inheritance which seals us until we have all of redemption's promises and experience complete freedom—all for the supreme glory and honor of God!

How should I live? In the power of the Holy Spirit, demonstrating His Fruit daily.

Galatians 5:22-24 The Message (MSG)

But what happens when we live God's way? He brings gifts into our lives, much the same way that fruit appears in an orchard—things like affection for others, exuberance about life, serenity. We develop a willingness to stick with things, a sense of compassion in the heart, and a conviction that a basic holiness permeates things and people. We find ourselves involved in loyal commitments, not needing to force our way in life, able to marshal and direct our energies wisely.

Conclusion:

And that's about it, friends. Be cheerful. Keep things in good repair. Keep your spirits up. Think in harmony. Be agreeable. Do all that, and the God of love and peace will be with you for sure. Greet one another with a holy embrace. All the brothers and sisters here say hello. The amazing grace of the Master, Jesus Christ, the extravagant love of God, the intimate friendship of the Holy Spirit, be with all of you. (2 Corinthians 13:11-14 The Message)

I close my letter with these last words: Be happy. Grow in Christ. Pay attention to what I have said. Live in harmony and peace. And may the God of love and peace be with you .Greet each other warmly in the Lord. All the Christians here send you their best regards. May the grace of our Lord Jesus Christ be with you all. May God's love and the Holy Spirit's friendship be yours. (2 Corinthians 13:11-14 The Living Bible)

CPSIA information can be obtained
at www.ICGtesting.com
Printed in the USA
BVHW061543290321
603636BV00014B/922

9 781662 811289